The GreedyPanda
COOK
BOOK

Essential Rice Cooker Recipes

YumAsia

written by rice cooker experts
for rice cooker enthusiasts

HAPPY
COOKING

Hardcover ISBN 978-1-9989971-2-1
Paperback ISBN 978-1-9989971-0-7
eBook ISBN 978-1-9989971-1-4

Printed by Yum Asia in the United Kingdom
www.yum-asia.com

3rd Edition, September 2022

CONTENTS

VEGETARIAN   5

MEAT   32

FISH 64

DESSERT 85

RICE GRAINS GUIDE

104

RICE COOKERS EXPLAINED

115

SLOW COOK AND STEAMING GUIDE

126

INDEX

128

INTRODUCTION

You love rice and need some inspiration to get cooking? This cook book covers the most popular rice dishes using a variety of grains and techniques along with some extra treats. When cooked correctly, rice on it's own can be delicious. Add good rice to your favourite main meal and it instantly becomes more interesting.

This book is about making great, simple and tasty food with the help from a rice cooker but the recipes can be made using normal everyday tools in a kitchen such as pots and pans. We would, however, advise that to get the best from your rice and the recipes in this book, having a good rice cooker would be helpful. Some recipes can be done entirely in a rice cooker whilst other recipes explain how to make perfect dishes that are usually served with rice. Basically, if you love rice then there will be a lot here for you.

We take you on a journey through a world of flavours from Indian dals to spicy, sweet and savoury Thai dishes to Chinese favourites and the sushi shores of Japan. We explore Mexican and Brazilian dishes, some European favourites, Middle Eastern delights, and everything in between. Along the way we give guidance and explain food tricks to get the most flavour from your cooking. We add information on how to pair dishes with rice, how to elevate rice to a higher level and explain how rice should be eaten!

We include recipes for interesting desserts you can make in a rice cooker, yes desserts! Whilst rice cookers are very good at cooking rice, the way that they operate means that they are also good at cooking specific key dishes that are more than just rice. We show how these can give variety to your cookery skills and maximise the potential of rice cooking.

Finally, we give interesting facts about rice, rice cookers, grain guides, handy tips and other useful information to help you on your journey to a healthier way to eat!

Congratulations! You are now a part of our rice cooker revolution!

MEASUREMENTS GUIDE
We keep things simple and metric

ESSENTIAL MEASUREMENTS

pinch - literally just a sprinkle (sometimes we will also use a few common expressions of measurements such as 'sprinkle', 'splash', 'handful' but they are self explanatory).

tsp - teaspoon or 5ml

tbsp - tablespoon or 15ml

cup - 237ml or 8 fl oz

rice measuring cup* - 180ml*

SOME USEFUL CONVERSIONS

1 cup = 8 fl oz
1 cup = 16 tbsp
1000ml = 1 litre or 34 fl oz
1ml = 1g
1000g = 1kg
3 tsp = 1 tbsp = 1/16 cup
6 tsp = 2 tbsp = 1/8 cup
12 tsp = 4 tbsp = ¼ cup
24 tsp = 8 tbsp = ½ cup
36 tsp = 12 tbsp = ¾ cup
48 tsp = 16 tbsp = 1 cup
1 cup = ½ pint
1 cup = ¼ quart
1 cup = 240ml

*Volume (rather than weight) of rice is the preferred method when measuring rice. Why?

This is because all rice has a different weight and when cooking rice it is important to be exact for rice cooking perfection! The weight varies depending on the grain type and the moisture in the grains. This means, for example ,that a full measuring cup of white jasmine rice may weigh very differently to a full cup of brown rice and so on. The weight can also vary between rice batch depending on how old or new the crop is.

THE RICE MEASURING CUP

The **gō** or cup is a traditional Japanese unit and is used for a serving of rice and a cup of sake in Japanese cuisine. Although the gō is no longer used as an official unit, 1-gō measuring cups or their **180ml** metric equivalents are often included with modern premium rice cookers.

1 gō ≈ 180ml ≈ 6.10 US fl oz ≈ ¾ metric cup

The scale on most rice measuring cups ends at 160ml but the capacity is actually 180ml. This is because you are supposed to fill the cup to the top (brim) with rice and level it off with chopsticks or a knife to get the full 180ml measurement. So when you fill with rice to get a full 180ml measuring cup...

**'Don't forget to go right to the brim
and then level off the rice'**

ADJUSTING FOR YOUR COOKER SIZE

Most of the ingredient quantities detailed can be used with any capacity rice cooker unless specifically mentioned. It's more important to think about how many people you will be making the recipe for and scale the ingredients if needed.

For example, if the recipe you are using serves 4 people but you are only cooking for 2 people you can either halve the ingredients or make enough for 4 and consider freezing the leftovers for another time. If the recipe serves 2 but you want to make enough food for 8 people then multiply the ingredient quantities four fold (x4).

If the recipe suggests to cook 2 rice measuring cups of rice but you have 4 people wanting rice then simply use 4 rice measuring cups of rice instead.

ICONS AND EQUIPMENT

The stuff that helps you use this book and cook

RECIPE ICON GUIDE

 Recipe will be spicy
Adjust to your taste

 Recipe is vegan

 Recipe uses a rice cooker**

 Number of servings

 Recipe uses a pan

 Cooking time in minutes

 **Note that although our recipes use rice cookers you can also use a saucepan and your stove cooker to perform similar tasks. However we would strongly recommend using a rice cooker as it reduces complication and helps you spend more time on meal preparation.

USEFUL COOKERY EQUIPMENT

 Rice Cooker - the key to perfect rice and makes the recipes contained in this book infinitely easier to cook.

 Pan/Wok - probably the most useful secondary tool to create a full rice meal that you need alongside your rice cooker.

 Rice Sieve - use this to remove small broken grains from your rice and/or use to rinse your rice to remove excess starch

 Mortar and Pestle - to grind those spices, herbs and powders together. Particulary helpful for pastes.

 Food Processor/Mixer - to quickly chop vegetables, leaves, making pastes etc. Not essential but time saving.

 Knives - a good knife or knife set is useful. We like Japanese steel knives but as long as it's sharp it will do the job.

 x2 Chopping Boards - use a high density plastic board for your onions, chillies, garlic. Use a wood board for everything else.

 Rice Moulding Bowl - any small bowl around size 11cm diameter and 5cm height is ideal. Put in the rice, press and turn upside down.

 Plate Set - a good plate set to show off your food. Use opposing colours to really set off the colours in whatever you have cooked.

 Measuring Equipment - a measuring spoon set and a measuring jug helps things go smoothly.

VEG

MEAT

CURATED FOR YOU

FEELING HUNGRY?

Recipes are sorted and
colour coded by meal type

FISH

DESSERT

VEGETARIAN

INDIAN PILAU RICE

Pilau rice or pilaf can be a fragrant side or showstopping main

 2/3   45"   EASY  RICE COOKER + PAN

Pilaf or pilau is a rice dish, or in some regions, a wheat dish. The recipe usually involves cooking in stock or broth, adding spices, and other ingredients such as vegetables or meat. The technique for cooking achieves rice grains that do not stick together.

INGREDIENTS

- **1 tbsp** groundnut or neutral oil
- **1 small** onion finely chopped
- **1 stick** cinnamon split lengthways
- **¾ tsp** cumin seeds, dry-toasted in a pan and crushed (or the same amount of cuminpowder)
- **2 pods** cardamom
- **2 tsp** ground tumeric
- **6** cloves
- **1 pinch** fresh thyme
- **2** bay leaves
- **2 rice measuring cups** basmati rice

HOW TO MAKE

1. Heat the oil in a large pan, add the onion and gently cook until softened.

2. Stir in the spices and herbs and cook for 1 minute then add the rice and stir until coated.

3. Transfer rice and spice/onion mix to your rice cooker bowl and add cold water to the level 2 white rice level line on the rice cooker inner bowl.

4. Close the lid, use the 'WHITE', 'REGULAR' or 'LONG GRAIN' function of your rice cooker and press 'START'.

5. Once cooked, open the lid, fluff up the rice with the spatula and remove the remaining whole pieces of spice.

HANDY TIP!

This pilau rice is a really easy side dish that you can whip up in no time with your rice cooker. This version is vegan and really delicious. We served this as part of a finger-food medley of samosas and pakora but it could be paired with curries or any other main dish that you want to add a bit more flavour to.

BUTTERNUT SQUASH RISOTTO

A satisfying veggie supper that uses a basic risotto recipe and gives it an autumnal twist

2   65"   MEDIUM   RICE COOKER + PAN

No standing over the stove top stirring this risotto – it's easy to do in your rice cooker!

INGREDIENTS

- **2 tbsp** olive oil
- **2 tbsp** butter (dairy or non-dairy)
- **2/3 cup** finely chopped yellow onion
- **1⅓ rice measuring cups** medium grain risotto rice (superfine Arborio, Carnaroli or Vialone nano)
- **1¾ cups** seeded and peeled butternut squash, cut into ½ inch cubes
- **1½ cups** water and **1½ cups** stock (any type)

TO FINISH

- **2 tsp** butter (dairy or non-dairy)
- **2 tbsp** lime juice
- **1½ cups** fresh chopped Italian parsley leaves

- **¼ cup** freshly grated parmesan cheese (dairy or non-dairy), plus more for serving
- **pinch** salt and pepper to taste

*You can also add diced courgette/zucchini, the flavour combines well with the butternut squash.

HOW TO MAKE

1. Place olive oil and butter in pan. When the butter melts add the onion, cook, stirring a few times until softened – about 2 minutes. Add rice and stir to coat the grains with hot butter/oil mixture. Cook, stirring a few times, until the grains of rice are transparent except for a spot of white on each one – about 3-5 minutes*

2. Add the rice, squash, water and stock to the inner bowl of your rice cooker and stir to combine. Close the cover and set the 'PORRIDGE' function for 1 hour.

3. When the machine switches to 'KEEP WARM', stir the risotto. There should only be a bit of liquid and the rice should be **al dente** – i.e. tender with a touch of resistance. If needed, cook for a few minutes longer. This risotto will keep on the keep warm setting for an hour, any longer and it will thicken considerably.

4. When ready to serve add the butter. Close the lid for a while to allow the butter to melt. Stir in lime juice, parsley, cheese and salt to taste and serve immediately.

   *You could do the first step (cooking and coating the onions/rice) in the rice cooker using 'QUICK COOK' or 'REGULAR' functions but you have to wait for the rice cooker to cool before you set the porridge setting otherwise a heat error will probably appear on the display.

PERSIAN TAHDIG WITH POTATOES

Known as scorched or crust rice in several countries

Tahdig, pronounced tah-deeg, literally means "bottom of the pot" in Persian This recipe could just be the beginning of rice more beautiful. Using the CRUST function of the rice cooker it is truly a taste sensation.

2/3   45"   EASY   RICE COOKER

INGREDIENTS

- ½ **medium** potato
- **2 rice measuring cups** long grain rice like basmati or jasmine
- **pinch** saffron
- **1 knob** butter (dairy or non-dairy)
- **pinches** salt and pepper
- **1 tsp** olive oil
- ½ onion finely sliced
- **1 clove** garlic, crushed

HOW TO MAKE

1. Finely slice the onion and crush the garlic. Fry in olive oil and leave to cool.

2. Cut the potato into thin slices. Arrange the sliced potato on the bottom of the inner bowl so it is fully is covered.

3. Add the 2 cups of rice on top of the potatoes (wash rice first if needed) then add water to the 2 cup mark for long grain.

4. Close the lid, select the 'CRUST' funtion and press and hold 'START'. **For this recipe we left the cooking time to the default 1 hour 30 mins.**

5. The rice cooker will beep after a while (this differs depending on how the fuzzy logic works out the cooking programme) which prompts you to add saffron, butter, onions and garlic and salt and pepper (or any other spices you want) and gently mix through.

6. Close the lid, to continue the cook cycle.

7. Once finished carefully tip the tahdig onto a plate and serve. The best way to do this is put the plate on top of the bowl like a lid, then using oven gloves or a tea towel, carefully tip the bowl upside down and the tahdig will fall easily onto the plate.

HANDY TIP! Best made with a minimum of 2 cups of rice but you can scale the recipe up to make more rice if you need. If you do cook the full capacity, you may need to set a longer cooking time. Ingredients commonly added to tahdig include yoghurt and saffron, bread, potato, tomato, and fruits such as sour cherry.

2/3   50"   EASY   RICE COOKER + PAN

SIMPLE EGG FRIED RICE

The classic Chinese rice dish perfected

A good egg fried rice dish should have a nice mix of egg through the rice, be well seasoned, together with the right amount of vegetables for a much needed crunch and to pack flavour into the dish.

INGREDIENTS

- **2 rice measuring cups** white jasmine rice
- **1 tbsp** vegetable oil
- **1** egg (whisked)
- **80g** petit pois peas
- **1-2 tbsp** light soy sauce
- **2 sticks** spring onions
- **pinches** black and white pepper

HANDY TIP! You can keep it authentic but make it more interesting by adding thin matchstick carrots and sliced tomatoes. Add depth of flavour with black pepper and a pinch of white pepper at the end.

HOW TO MAKE

1. Add rice to your rice cooker bowl and fill up to level 2 white rice line with water. Select the 'LONG GRAIN', 'REGULAR' or 'WHITE' function. Once cooked, allow the rice to cool down for 30 minutes minimum (a few hours in a sealed container in a fridge is best).

2. Whisk the egg with a fork until smooth whilst your pan (ideally a good wok) is heating to a very high temperature. Then add ½ tbsp of vegetable oil until it reaches smoking-point (**aka - wok hei**)

3. Pour in the egg and stir whilst it's cooking. Get the egg partially crispy then turn the heat down by ⅓. Push the egg to one side and add another ½ tbsp of vegetable oil. Bring the wok back to a high heat.

4. Add the cooled rice to the wok and mix well with the egg. Remove clumps. Once mixed add the peas and stir-fry for 1 minute.

5. Add the soy sauce and sesame oil and turn the heat down by 1/3 again. Stir fry until the rice absorbs all the liquid (about 1 minute).

6. Once the rice are 'dancing' around the bottom of the wok, your rice is ready to serve. Garnish with more spring onion if required.

MASOOR DAL TADKA

A yummy red lentil dal with all the aromatics

HANDY TIP! Garnish with fresh coriander and for a pretty effect you can drizzle plain yoghurt in a concentric pattern. This is not good for vegans however!

6   30"   EASY   RICE COOKER + PAN

Tadka is a cooking method where spices and other aromatics are cooked briefly in hot oil to bring out their best flavour. Full of nutrients and naturally vegan...it's a nutritious meal.

INGREDIENTS

- **2 rice measuring cups** dry masoor dal (aka red lentils), sorted and well rinsed
- **4 rice measuring cups** water
- **3 rice measuring cups** basmati rice (to serve)
- **400g** diced fresh tomatoes/tin of tomatoes
- **1 tbsp** coconut or neutral flavoured oil
- **1 large** yellow onion (finely diced)
- **1 tbsp** minced ginger
- **¼ tsp** ground cumin
- **1 tsp** whole mustard seeds
- **1 tsp** ground coriander
- **1 tbsp** Indian curry powder
- **2** green chillies (take out seeds if you want less heat)
- **pinches** salt to taste

HOW TO MAKE

1. Combine the lentils and water in your rice cooker bowl. Use the 'SLOW COOK' function and cook for 30 minutes.

2. While the lentils are cooking, make the tadka by adding the oil, onion, garlic, ginger, chillies and a pinch of salt to a heated pan. Fry until soft (about 5 mins).

3. Add the spices: curry powder, mustard seeds, coriander, and cumin, along with a pinch of salt.

4. Mix and cook for about 60 seconds, then add the tomatoes. Cook for about 7 minutes to reduce.

5. Open your rice cooker then add the tadka to the cooked lentils, and leave on keep warm for around 20 minutes to infuse with flavour and release the aromatics. The longer you leave it, the richer the flavour.

6. Serve with basmati rice.

SPICY MEXICAN RICE

A great companion dish to any Mexican main or just eat it alone and it's equally yummy

4   80"   MEDIUM   RICE COOKER + PAN

The jalapeno chillies give a lovely smokey but subtle spicy flavour and cooking it in your Yum Asia rice cooker makes it even easier!

A great side dish which is vegetarian and vegan – best of all your leftovers can be used the next day to make 'Mexican fried rice', just fry in the same way you would normal cold rice and it's a delicious twist to a lunchtime staple.

INGREDIENTS

- **2 rice measuring cups** long grain rice
- **1 clove** of garlic (crushed)
- **1** red onion (thinly sliced)
- **1** jalapeno chilli (chopped finely, seeds left in – depends on how spicy you like it!). You can substitute fresh with 'from a jar' if you wish
- **1 tin** (400ml) tomatoes (we strain and push this through a sieve to just get the liquid, but you could use 200ml passata instead)
- **1 cube** vegetable stock
- **100ml** hot water
- **pinches** black pepper and salt

HOW TO MAKE

1. Put two cups of rice in a bowl and cover with boiling water. Leave for 10 minutes. Drain, rinse with cold water and leave to drain.

2. Put 1 tsp of olive oil in a pan and fry the garlic, onion and jalapeno.

3. Once slightly browned add the rice and fry until it's dried out and turning slightly golden.

4. Add the rice, garlic, onion and jalapeno to the rice cooker bowl and then pour the tomato juice on top.

5. Stir well, add a shake of pepper and the stock cube and water. If necessary, top up with water to between the 2 and 3 cup level line for white rice.

6. Close the lid and press 'START' (use normal 'WHITE', 'REGULAR' or 'LONG GRAIN' rice function).

7. When the cooking cycle is complete, lift the lid, it will look wet. Stir the rice to release the steam and moisture and leave on keep warm for at least 30 minutes – this will dry the rice and intensify the flavour.

HANDY TIP! Add a handful of frozen/fresh peas at the beginning of the cooking cycle to add extra flavour and colour. For meat lovers this pairs well with fajitas!

FRITTATA IN A RICE COOKER

Fluffy, creamy, protein, carbs
and vegetables all done in a rice cooker

4   **50"**   **EASY**   **RICE COOKER + PAN**

You see, the secret to a great frittata is that you use a rice cooker!
Good on it's own or even better in some fresh bread or baguette.
This recipe is a great example of the versatility of a rice cooker.

INGREDIENTS

- **1 whole** garlic clove (squashed with flat of knife)
- ¼ red onion diced
- ¼ red pepper, ¼ yellow pepper diced
- **1 small** potato finely diced
- **2** spring onions
- **6** cherry tomatoes (halved)
- **pinches** salt and pepper
- **1 tbsp** olive oil
- **6** eggs
- **2 tbsp** grated cheese

HOW TO MAKE

1. Heat the frying pan with 1 tbsp olive oil and fry the garlic to release the flavour (when it's brown take it out).

2. Add the onions and fry until soft. Add the finely diced potato and pepper, fry for 4-5 minutes. Add the cherry tomatoes and spring onions and fry for another 2-3 minutes. Season with salt and pepper.

3. While cooking the above vegetables, whisk the eggs in a bowl and add a generous amount of salt and pepper.

4. Grease the inner bowl of the rice cooker with a small amount of olive oil (use kitchen paper to ensure a good, even coverage)

5. Put the cooked vegetables into the inner bowl and then pour the eggs on top. Add the cheese and stir with a plastic or silicone spoon. Make sure the vegetables are distributed evenly through the egg mixture.

7. Close the lid, choose the 'REGULAR' 'WHITE' or 'LONG GRAIN' rice function and press 'START'

8. When the cooking cycle is finished, tip out onto a plate, cut into quarters and serve with a fresh baguette and mixed salad.

HANDY TIP! Add whatever vegetables you want to this one. Can be stored well wrapped in a fridge for 2-3 days or put in your bento for a good filling lunch!

PEARL BARLEY AND VEGETABLE SOUP

Filling, nutritious and versatile soup

2/3 | **150"** | **EASY** | **RICE COOKER + PAN**

This is a very versatile and forgiving soup. You can literally throw any vegetables that you have into it, the more veg the better. Let your rice cooker soften the pearl barley to perfection whilst stewing the vegetables to release the flavour.

INGREDIENTS

- **1 large** red onion – chopped into chunks
- **¾ cup** pearl barley (washed)
- **2 medium** carrots
- **1** bell pepper (whatever colour you have) chopped into chunks
- **8 sticks** green beans chopped into smaller pieces
- **4 sticks** baby sweetcorn chopped into smaller pieces
- **2 sticks** broccoli stalks, sliced (optional), leafy green veg (cabbage, spinach, brocolli leaves) set aside
- **5 stock cubes** dissolved in 1 litre of hot water
- **400ml** hot water
- **1 dash** olive oil
- **5 pinches** salt, black pepper, white pepper, **1 tsp** of dried tarragon, **1 tsp** of oregano, **a pinch** of cayenne pepper.

  *optional non veggie option - add 2 chicken breasts cut in half (if you want to substitute with cooked chicken, that's okay too)

HOW TO MAKE

1. Add a little olive oil to a pan and add the onions. Fry for 5 minutes.

2. When the onions are beginning to turn translucent, add the veg (apart from the leafy greens) and cook for a further 5 minutes.

3. Remove the vegetables from the pan, add to the rice cooker inner bowl with the pearl barley

4. ****For a meat version you would brown the chicken at this point.**** Add the whole of the stock to the inner bowl and add seasoning

5. Mix all the ingredients together well and add the additional water.

6. Close the lid and select the 'SLOW COOK' or 'SOUP' function. Press 'START' then cook for at least 2 hours.

7. 20 minutes before you are ready to serve adjust the seasoning and add the leafy veg. If you are having the meat version you can shred the chicken (take out of the inner bowl to do this!) and add back to the soup

HANDY TIP! Serve with big chunks of sourdough bread which mops up the savoury soup perfectly. This recipe freezes very well, so don't worry about having too much – you have an easy soup ready to defrost and reheat.

MALAY NASI LEMAK

This staple is often eaten for breakfast in Malaysia
but is suitable at any time of day

| 2 | 70" | EASY | RICE COOKER + PAN |

The basic elements of any good nasi lemak tend to be coconut rice, ikan bilis (mini fried anchovies) and sambal (a sort of hot, spicy, chilli paste) topped with peanuts, cucumber and egg. The different textures when plated is what makes this one stand out. Remove the anchovies and this can be a very effective vegetarian dish.

INGREDIENTS FOR THE SAMBAL

12 dried chillies soaked in hot water
2 small onions (or 5 shallots) finely chopped
½ **tbsp** tamarind dissolved in 2 tsp of water
2 tbsp vegetable oil
1 tsp sugar and ½ **tsp** of salt.

FOR THE RICE

2 rice measuring cups white long grain rice
1 rice measuring cup stock (vegetable or chicken)
1 rice measuring cup coconut milk

FOR THE TOPPINGS

peanuts
sliced cucumber
ikan bilis (optional and non vegetarian salt-cured anchovies)
1 hard boiled egg (optional)

HANDY TIP! You can also try serving with Sambal Kacang Goreng (green bean sambal). This is a classic Malay dish after all, but even classics have variety.

HOW TO MAKE

1. Drain the chillies then blend with the onions/shallots and half of the tamarind mixture until smooth

2. Fry the paste off with the oil in a saucepan over a low heat for 10 minutes until fragrant and darker in colour.

3. Add the sugar, salt and the rest of the tamarind then simmer for 5 minutes.

4. Place two cups of white rice in your rice cooker bowl and fill to the 'WHITE/LONG GRAIN RICE' level 2 with 1 cup of coconut milk and 1 cup of stock (vegetable or chicken).

5. Select the 'WHITE RICE', 'LONG GRAIN' or 'REGULAR' funtion. Press 'START'.

6. Leave on 'KEEP WARM' for 10 minutes for the rice to suck up some of the tasty moisture.

7. For the toppings, Fry some peanuts (skins on preferably) in a little oil until brown.

8. Serve with a helping of the sambal, peanuts, slices of fresh cucumber and a hard boiled egg.

4 · 70" · EASY · RICE COOKER + PAN

ALOO GOBI WITH A KICK

Potatoes and cauliflower cooked with onion, tomatoes & spices

Aloo Gobi is one of the most popular dishes in Indian cuisine. It is made using two main ingredients - potatoes (aloo) and cauliflower (gobi). Commonly cooked with tomatoes and a selection of aromatics and warm spices that are simply magical when put together in this incredibly simple yet effective recipe.

● INGREDIENTS

4 rice measuring cups basmati rice
400g floury potatoes (such as Maris Piper or King Edward), cut into medium-sized chunks
1 large cauliflower, cut into florets
2 tins chopped tomatoes (400g each)
1 tbsp cumin seeds
2 tsp coriander seeds
2 tsp nigella seeds
1 tsp ground cinnamon
1 tsp turmeric
1 tsp chilli powder
8 curry leaves
4 cloves crushed garlic
2 small green chillies, pierced a few times
4 sticks coriander, chopped
1 juiced lime
1 tsp golden caster sugar
4 tbsp vegetable oil or sunflower oil or rapeseed oil

HANDY TIP! You want the veg to be cooked and tender but not soggy. To keep cauliflower consistency don't cover the pan when cooking. If you need to cover do so on a low heat at the end of cooking only.

● HOW TO MAKE

1. Add the rice to your rice cooker inner bowl and fill to the level 4 white rice line with water. Select the 'WHITE RICE', 'LONG GRAIN' or 'REGULAR' function and press 'START'.

2. Tip the potatoes into a large pan, fill with cold water and bring to the boil

3. Simmer for 5-6 mins until starting to soften but still holding their shape. Drain well.

4. Put the potatoes and cauliflower with the spices and 2 tbsp oil and shallow fry until they are golden and the vegetables become soft.

5. In a separate pan fry the curry leaves and garlic for 1 min, making sure the garlic doesn't brown.

6. Add the tomatoes, chillies, sugar, lime juice and some seasoning. Cover with a lid and simmer for 15 mins until the tomatoes have broken down.

7. Add the toasted veg to the tomatoes. Simmer for 5 mins, adding a splash of water if the curry gets too thick.

8. Stir through the coriander and serve with naan bread (yoghurt if you wish) and basmati rice.

VEGETABLE LASAGNE

An alternative to the usual bake with this low calorie version of an Italian favourite

4 **150"** **MEDIUM** **RICE COOKER**

Layered with pasta, ratatouille, cheese and sliced aubergine this healthier take on the Italian favourite packs in all of your five-a-day and more. All made in a rice cooker using the SLOW COOK function.

INGREDIENTS

- **400 g (or 1 tin)** chopped tomatoes
- **1 tbsp** rapeseed oil
- **1** red pepper (de-seeded and roughly sliced) and **1** yellow pepper (de-seeded and roughly sliced)
- **2 large** courgettes, diced (400g)
- **1 large** aubergine, sliced across length or width for maximum surface area
- **2** onions, sliced
- **2 tbsp** tomato purée
- **9 (150g)** lasagne sheets - wholewheat works well
- **125g** vegetarian buffalo mozzarella, chopped (add some mature cheddar if you want more flavour)
- **FOR THE FLAVOUR**
  ½ **tsp** oregano
  ½ **tsp** thyme
  3 tsp vegetable bouillon
  2 large garlic cloves, chopped
  15g fresh basil, chopped plus a few leaves

HANDY TIP! Add some chilli flakes to the mixture if you like a zing in your lasagna. Mature cheddar works well to cut through the flavour.

HOW TO MAKE

1. Heat 1 tbsp rapeseed oil in non-stick pan and fry 2 sliced onions with 2 chopped large garlic cloves for 5 mins, stirring frequently until soft.

2. Add 2 diced large courgettes, peppers with 400g chopped tomatoes with 2 tbsp tomato purée, 2 tsp vegetable bouillon and 15g chopped basil.

3. Stir well with the oregano and thyme cover then cook for 5 mins. Don't be tempted to add more liquid as plenty of moisture will come from the vegetables once they start cooking.

4. Slice 1 large aubergine. Lay half of it in the base of the cooker bowl and top with 3 lasagne sheets.

5. Add a third of the ratatouille mixture, then the remaining aubergine slices, 3 more lasagne sheets, then the remaining mixture to make a layering effect in the bowl. Stack the layers as high as you like.

6. Select the 'SLOW COOK' function , set the cooking time for 90-120 minutes to soften the vegetable.

7. Sprinkle mozzarella over the vegetables then cover and leave for 10 mins to settle and melt the cheese.

8. Garnish with basil and serve with some rocket.

PAELLA VERDURA

A vegetarian twist on this Spanish classic rice dish with the help of a rice cooker!

4   **70"**   **MEDIUM**   **RICE COOKER + PAN**

Paella full of vegetables can be made quickly with the help of a rice cooker. A brief use of a pan after baking is the key to achieving a crispy rice crust on the bottom, often referred to as socarrat (meaning "burnt" in Catalan).

INGREDIENTS

- **4 tbsp** extra-virgin olive oil
- **2 medium** courgette, halved lengthwise and sliced into half moons
- **225g** sliced mushrooms
- **pinch** salt
- **½ small** yellow onion, finely chopped
- **3 cloves** garlic, finely chopped
- **1 tsp** smoked paprika
- **pinch** saffron threads (optional)
- **1 tin (400g)** chopped tomatoes
- **2 rice measuring cups** short-grain uncooked paella rice (such as Bomba rice)
- **140g** fresh or frozen peas
- **140g** piquillo peppers, sliced (or roasted red peppers)
- **140g** baby spinach
- **800ml** vegetable stock
- **handful** fresh parsley, chopped for serving
- **4** lemon wedges, for serving

HOW TO MAKE

1. In a deep pan heat 2 tbsp oil over medium heat. Add courgette and mushrooms and season with salt. Cook, until golden on one side, about 3 minutes. Toss and cook, stirring occasionally, until golden and tender, 8 to 10 minutes; transfer to a small bowl.

2. To same pan, add 2 tbsp olive oil and return to medium heat. Add onion and season with salt. Cook, stirring often, until softened, 3 to 5 minutes. Add garlic, smoked paprika, and saffron and cook, stirring, until fragrant, 30 seconds.

3. Add tomatoes, ¾ teaspoon salt and the rice then stir to combine. Stir in courgette mixture, peas, piquillo peppers, and spinach, stirring to wilt spinach. Put this mixture into your rice cooker bowl, add stock so it comes to the level 2 'SHORT GRAIN' level line. Select the 'SHORT GRAIN' function and press 'START' (alternatively you can leave in the pan for 30 to 40 minutes or bake in a preheated oven set to 220°C).

4. Once the rice has finished cooking, if you want the crisp bottom, transfer to a pan and cook on the stovetop over medium heat to make sure the bottom of the rice is crisp - 2 to 3 minutes.

5. Let it rest for 5 minutes. Top with parsley and serve with lemon wedges.

HANDY TIP! For more crunch you can add some long thin green beans or tinned sweetcorn. Don't stir the paella when it's cooking in the oven or the pan. The idea is to preserve the status of the broth and rice to give a good soccarat (golden crust).

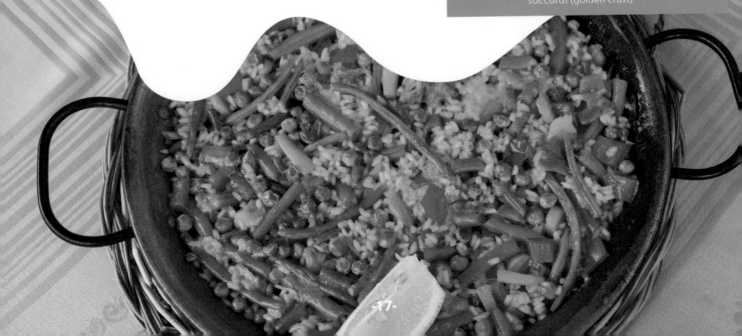

COCONUT GINGER RICE

Rich with coconut flavour, incredibly easy to throw together

2/3   55"   EASY   RICE COOKER

Coconut ginger rice is prepared by cooking white rice in coconut milk or coconut flakes. As both the coconut and the rice plant are indigenous in places all around the world, coconut rice too is found in many cultures spanning across the equator from the Caribbean to South-East Asia. This recipe adds the warmth of ginger to enhance this popular rice dish.

INGREDIENTS

- **2 rice measuring cups** long grain white rice
- **1 tsp** minced ginger (fresh or jar is fine)
- **125ml** vegetable stock
- **1 tin (400ml)** coconut milk
- **1 pinch** salt
- **1 dash** lemon or lime juice
- **1** Thai chili finely chopped (for garnish, can be left out)
- **3 sticks** spring onions (scallions) finely chopped (for garnish, can be left out)

HOW TO MAKE

1. Place 2 cups of rice in your rice cooker inner bowl, add coconut milk, stock, salt and ginger. Make sure it comes to the long grain mark labelled 2 on the inner bowl.

2. Select the 'LONG GRAIN' , 'REGULAR' or 'WHITE' rice function then press the 'START' button.

3. Once the cooking cycle has finished, stir the rice and leave it on keep warm setting for 15 minutes.

4. Just before you are ready to serve add a squirt of lime/lemon juice and add spring onions and chilli to garnish, if you are using it.

HANDY TIP! Coconut rice is the anchor of Nasi Lemak, Malaysia's national dish. Serve with Piri Piri Chicken (subsitute for Tofu if you like) for a more interesting rice accompaniment.

BAO BUNS IN A RICE COOKER

Fluffy soft steamed buns – experience the flavour of Asian street food

4   50"   MEDIUM   RICE COOKER

For many centuries in Asia the simple bao bun has been popular and recently this delicious treat has become a popular staple in restaurants all over the world. Use your rice cooker 'STEAM' function for optimal cooking of this doughy delight.

INGREDIENTS

- **530g** middle gluten wheat flour (alternatively, plain flour/all-purpose flour), plus extra for dusting
- **½ tsp** salt
- **7g** fast action dried yeast
- **40g** caster sugar
- **15g** baking powder
- **50ml** milk
- **200 - 250ml** warm water (depending on how humid your room is. Add more water if room is dry)
- **25ml** vegetable or sunflower oil

HOW TO MAKE

1. Put the dry ingredients into the bowl of a free-standing mixer fitted with a dough hook attached (if available).

2. Mix the liquid ingredients together into a measuring jug. Slowly pour the liquid into the mixer while kneading on a low speed for around 2 minutes until all the water is mixed into the flour. Once mixed turn the speed up to high for a further 2 minutes until the dough has a smooth yet tacky feel to it.

3. Once the dough has been well kneaded, dust with 2 tbsp of flour, scraping off any extra dough on the sides of the bowl.

4. Shape the dough into a ball and coat it with 1 tbsp of vegetable oil. Put the dough back into the bowl.

5. Cover with a damp cloth in a warm, preferably moist, draft-free location (such as inside a room temperature oven) for 1–1.5 hours.

6. Once the dough has doubled in size, you can then shape it into whatever shape you wish before steaming.

7. Fill your rice cooker bowl to the white rice level 2 line and place the buns into your steaming basket.

8. Close lid and press 'STEAM'. Steaming time will vary between 10–15 minutes depending on the shape and size of your finished buns (the thinner the bun, the shorter the steaming time).

HANDY TIP! For fillings you could use crispy chicken or duck, BBQ tofu/seitan or tempeh, pan fried mushrooms and chives, braised pork belly....the choice is yours.

-19-

INDONESIAN NASI GORENG

An important staple enjoyed
at breakfast, buffets or
when on the go

 1-2   60"   **EASY**  **RICE COOKER + PAN**

Nasi Goreng, literally meaning "fried rice" in Indonesian, is a filling main and works well with any protein of your choice. Use tofu if you want a vegetarian version or just go without meat for an equally tasty meal.

INGREDIENTS

- **1 rice measuring cup** long grain rice
- **1** egg
- **¼** red pepper
- **2** spring onions
- **1 clove** garlic
- **1 tsp** shrimp paste (optional or use veg shrimp paste if available. You can also substitue fermented soy paste or miso)
- **2 tbsp** sweet soy sauce (also known as kecap manis)
- **dash** sesame oil
- **1 tsp** salt (Or to taste)
- sambal **to taste**
- **handful** tofu (optional - or meat if you wish)

HOW TO MAKE

1. Add the rice to your rice cooker inner bowl and fill with water to the 1 rice level line. Select the rice function for the rice you are cooking and press 'START'. Leave to cool.

2. Finely chop the spring onions, dice the red pepper and chop the garlic.

3. Heat 1 tbsp vegetable oil in a wok. Add the garlic and peppers to the wok and stir fry for 1 minute. Push aside to allow space for the rest of the ingredients.

4. Heat 1 tbsp vegetable oil in a wok on high heat. Crack the egg into the wok and fry. Once the egg is half cooked, break the yolk and cut into the white with your spatula. Push the egg to one side of the wok to allow space for your rice.

5. Separate the cooked rice using a spatula. Add 1 tbsp vegetable oil to the wok and when smoking hot, add the rice then mix well. Add 1 tsp shrimp paste and 2 tbsp sweet soy sauce (kecap manis) to the pan.

6. Continue to stir fry and make sure the paste and soy sauce get well mixed into the rice. Add salt and pepper to taste. Finally add a dash of sesame oil and stir. Serve and garnish with spring onion on the top.

 HANDY TIP! To add texture to this beautiful dish, serve with prawn crackers on the side and some diced cucumber to cleanse the palate between bites

2   75"   EASY   RICE COOKER

COCONUT LIME DAL

A zingy dal perfect when served with naan and rice

Dal (also spelled dhal or daal) is one of the most versatile, healthy, filling, and delicious meals Dal translates to lentil, but when referred to in the context of food it means a spiced Indian lentil soup. This is a colourful, zingy and easy to make dal - perfect for dipping and makes even the most simple servings of rice instantly more interesting.

INGREDIENTS

- **150g** red lentils, rinsed
- **¼ tsp** ground turmeric
- **1 tin (400ml)** coconut milk
- **200ml** boiling water
- **90g** fresh coconut chunks (cut into 1cm cubes)
- **1 clove** garlic
- **1 stick** spring onion chopped finely
- **1 tsp** ground cumin
- **1 tbsp** vegetable oil
- **3 big handfuls** of baby leaf spinach
- **pinch** sea salt to taste
- **1 whole** lime, juiced and zested

HOW TO MAKE

1. Add the lentils, turmeric, coconut milk, coconut pieces, boiling water and garlic to your rice cooker inner bowl.

2. Mix the cumin, spring onion and oil on a chopping board. Scatter over the lentils.

3. Close the lid and press the 'SLOW COOK' function. Set the cooking time for 60 minutes then press 'START'

4. Once cooked open the rice cooker and stir in the spinach leaves until they wilt slightly. Adjust texture with boiling water.

5. Stir in the lime juice including the zest. Adjust to taste with salt.

6. Serve with rice, naan bread or chapatis and extra wedges of lime for squeezing.

HANDY TIP! Fresh coconut pieces can usually be found in small vacuum packets in the chiller cabinet at the supermarket (normally near the cut-up pineapple and melon). This is easier than chopping up a whole coconut.

MIDDLE EASTERN TABBOULEH

A super fresh herb and bulgur salad, with bulgur, parsley and mint being the primary ingredients

3   40"   EASY   RICE COOKER

Tabbouleh is a Middle Eastern/North African salad made mostly of finely chopped parsley, with tomatoes, mint, onion, bulgur, and seasoned with olive oil, lemon juice and salt. Some variations add lettuce, or use semolina instead of bulgur. Tabbouleh is traditionally served as part of a mezze.

INGREDIENTS

- **1 cup** uncooked course bulgur wheat (equals 3 cups cooked)
- **4** firm Roma tomatoes, very finely chopped
- **1** cucumber, very finely chopped (remove skin if you prefer)
- **4 sticks** parsley, part of the stems removed, washed and well-dried, very finely chopped
- **12** fresh mint leaves, stems removed, washed, well-dried, very finely chopped
- **4 sticks** spring onions, white and green parts, finely chopped
- **pinch** salt
- **3 tbsp** lime juice (lemon juice, if you prefer)
- **3 tbsp** extra virgin olive oil
- **handful** romaine lettuce leaves to serve, optional
- ¼ red onion (optional)

HOW TO MAKE

1. Put 1 cup of course bulgar wheat into your rice cooker inner bowl, add 1.5 cups of water (measured in the rice cooker measuring cup).

2. Cook using the 'QUICK COOK', 'REGULAR', or 'LONG GRAIN' function of your rice cooker then press 'START'. Set aside to cool.

3. Very finely chop the tomatoes, cucumber, herbs and spring onions. Place the tomatoes in a colander to drain excess juice.

4. Place the chopped vegetables, herbs and spring onions in a mixing bowl.

5. Add the bulgur and season with salt. Mix gently.

6. Add the the lime juice and olive oil and mix again.

7. Taste and adjust the seasoning if needed.

HANDY TIP!

To make a marvellous mezze, combine with pita and romaine lettuce leaves to be used as wraps for the tabbouleh along with hummus, baba ghanoush, roasted red pepper hummus and falafel. Add pomegranate seeds to give an interesting texture/taste.

MIXED VEGETABLE TOMATO RICE

A satisfying veggie side dish that is really easy to prepare

2   50"   EASY   RICE COOKER

This is a super-easy and delicious recipe that can be served as a tasty side dish to a main meal or as a healthy lunch.

Often described as a 'steamed fried rice' it's very popular in Asia. You can add anything you want – vegetables, ham, other meat, tofu and any kinds of seasonings you want.

INGREDIENTS

- **2 rice measuring cups** long or short grain rice
- **1** tomato (skin peeled off)
- ½ carrot (chopped)
- ¼ different colour peppers (chopped)
- **1 cup** frozen peas

HOW TO MAKE

1. Put 2 cups of rice into the inner bowl (use the provided measuring cup). Fill to the corresponding line on the bowl with water.

2. Place the peeled tomato in the middle of the bowl on top of the rice and water. Add the other chopped vegetables on top.

3. Close the lid and select 'LONG GRAIN' (white) or 'SHORT GRAIN' function (for whichever type of rice you are using), close the lid and press 'START'

4. When the rice cooker beeps, lift the lid and break the tomato up and mix the rice and cooked vegetables together.

5. Add soy sauce, black or white pepper and any other seasoning you want to add at this point.

6. Mix into the rice and vegetables well.

7. Serve as a tasty side dish to a main meal or for a healthy lunch.

HANDY TIP!

Seasoning is the key here. Get it wrong and it can result in bland rice.

Even just a tomato placed on top of the rice at the beginning of cooking can taste great if seasoned correctly.

23

FULLY LOADED JACKET POTATOES

Smoky flavours combined with savoury delight

| 4 | 70-120" | EASY | RICE COOKER |

Baked potatoes can be made in a rice cooker using the 'SLOW COOK' function. By using this sealed cooking method you get softer potatoes with enhanced flavour and it uses less energy too than other heating methods because the rice cooker is a sealed unit as compared to a conventional slow cooker which usually has a loose fitting glass lid. Cook either small baby potatoes or go large with full size jackets then stuff with the alchemy of savoury and creamy blend to give a yummy flavour.

INGREDIENTS*

- **1 ½ lbs** baby (or small) potatoes, sliced in half. Use larger potatoes if you want full jackets

- **½ cup** milk or unsweetened oat milk

- **4 sticks** spring onion

- **½ tbsp** chilli powder

- **½ tbsp** smoked paprika

- **½ cup bacon bits** (use real smoked bacon or bacon flavoured bits). You can use vegan bacon if preferred.

- **¼ tsp** salt

- **OPTIONAL CHEESE ADD ON**

  100g grated mature cheddar cheese (or similar). For vegan you can use vegan cheese.

*Measurements are for a 5.5 cup capacty rice cooker. Scale accordingly for other rice cooker sizes.

HANDY TIP! If using big potatoes remember to prick them with a fork. Leave the skins on for extra nutrition (wash well first) and give the bigger potatoes more time. For extra melting of the cheese just stick them under a grill to bake further.

HOW TO MAKE

1. Lightly coat the inner bowl of your rice cooker with olive oil.

2. Place the sliced or baby potatoes, half of the spring onions, milk, smoked paprika, chilli powder and season with salt (use whole potatoes with skin left on instead of baby potatoes if you want to serve as full jacket potatoes).

3. Close the lid and select the 'SLOW COOK' function. Press 'START' for baby potatoes to cook for one hour or set the time to 2-3 hours for the larger jacket potatoes

   Stir/turn every 15-30 minutes to ensure even cooking.

4. Once finished cooking put the potatoes into a large serving bowl and top with cheese, sour cream, bacon bits, and the remaining chopped scallions.

   The chilli powder combined with smoked paprika and salt give a smoky kick for a perfect balance to the creamy cheese and sour cream if you use these. The fresh spring onions add a fresh crispness and the bacon bits contribute a savoury, smoky bite that melds the whole dish together.

YUMMY PIZZA RICE

Using tomato rice as a base with a pizza topping makes this hybrid recipe a winner

2/3   55"   EASY   RICE COOKER + PAN

This is pizza with a different carb because it uses rice instead of bread. You don't need to wait for that dough to proof and rise but is still delicious. Customize any way you want and use whatever kind of rice you want along with whatever cheese and toppings you want.

• FOR THE FRIED RICE

2 tbsp extra-virgin olive oil, divided
5 cloves garlic, quartered
¾ tsp onion powder
½ tsp freshly ground black pepper
½ tsp salt
½ tsp crushed red pepper flakes (optional)
¾ tsp Italian seasoning
2 tbsp tomato paste
¼ tsp freshly ground nutmeg (optional)
3 rice measuring cups cooked rice
½ cup freshly grated parmesan
1 tbsp sesame seeds (optional)

• FOR THE SAUCE

1 (400ml) tin crushed tomatoes
1 large clove garlic, grated
¼ tsp coarsely ground black pepper
1 tsp salt
¼ tsp crushed red pepper flakes
1 tbsp granulated sugar

• FOR THE TOPPING

1 cup mozzarella, shredded or whole
¼ cup freshly grated parmesan
½ cup pepperoni (non veg option)
handful fresh basil leaves

HOW TO MAKE

1. Make the plain rice first then in a 24cm oven-safe pan over medium heat add 1 tbsp oil. Then add garlic, onion, pepper, salt, red pepper flakes, and Italian seasoning, and cook until garlic turns golden (around 2 minutes).

2. Add tomato paste and cook until slightly caramelised (about 1 minute). Add nutmeg, remaining 1 tbsp oil, and rice, and cook until rice begins to turn slightly crispy, about 8 minutes. Reduce heat to the lowest setting, then stir in ½ cup parmesan and sesame seeds (if using) until well combined.

3. Preheat oven to 200°C / 400°F. To make the sauce, stir together all the sauce ingredients in a medium bowl until well combined.

4. To assemble the 'pizza': in a deep'ish pan spread ½ cup tomato sauce over fried rice in an even layer, then sprinkle mozzarella and parmesan evenly across, and top with pepperoni.

5. Transfer the pan to the oven and bake until the cheese is melty and edges are golden (about 10 minutes. Garnish with basil before serving.

HANDY TIP!

An oven and pan cooking is really needed for parts of this recipe to get the crispiness associated with pizza to happen.

This recipe is ideal for gluten free diets or anyone who wants to reduce the amount of bread / dough in their meals.

For the meat eaters you can add pepperoni, chicken, beef or fish and go to town for a protein hit.

MEDITERRANEAN QUINOA SALAD

This one is very quick to do,
fresh and tasty

3   **30"**   **EASY**   **RICE COOKER**

A healthy but absolutely delicious lunch or dinner side dish which is packed with delicious and fresh veg and herbs.

INGREDIENTS

- **1 cup** uncooked quinoa (equals 3 cups cooked)
  3 cups cherry tomatoes (roasted with some extra virgin olive oil and salt and pepper)
  2 cups arugula
  1 cup cucumber, sliced or chopped (preferably skin off)
  1 cup mixed basil and mint
  ¾ cup black olives, pitted and sliced
  ½ cup diced red onion
  ⅓ cup toasted pine nuts
  ½ tsp sea salt
  pinch freshly ground black pepper
  2 pinches chilli flakes (optional)
  1 cup roasted chickpeas
  'Italian' dressing (see below), plus 2 additional garlic cloves, grated/crushed

- **ITALIAN DRESSING**
  ¼ cup extra-virgin olive oil
  2 tbsp white wine vinegar
  2 tbsp lemon juice
  1 tbsp finely chopped fresh parsley
  1 tsp honey (or maple syrup to make it vegan)
  1 tsp dried oregano
  1 clove garlic grated
  ½ tsp Dijon mustard
  ½ tsp thyme
  ¼ tsp sea salt
  pinches freshly ground black pepper

HOW TO MAKE

1. Put 1 cup of quinoa into your rice cooker inner bowl and add 1 cup of water (measured in the rice cooker measuring cup).

2. Cook using the 'QUICK COOK' or 'WHITE RICE' or 'LONG GRAIN' function. Press 'START' then once finished cooking set aside to cool.

3. In a large bowl, combine the cooled quinoa, roasted tomatoes, arugula, cucumbers, herbs, olives, onion, and pine nuts.

4. Stir gently to combine, then drizzle with the dressing and stir again.

5. Add salt, pepper, chilli flakes if using, and stir again.

6. Top with the roasted chickpeas and serve.

7. Add any extra salt, pepper or lemon juice to taste.

HANDY TIP! The quinoa, roasted tomatoes and chickpeas can be made up to 3 days in advance and stored in the fridge until ready to use. For intense colour use 3 colour quinoa but remember to use slightly more water – 1:1.25 ratio would be ideal

4 40" EASY RICE COOKER

CREAMY MAC AND CHEESE

Macaroni and cheese (mac and cheese) is popular as a quick snack or main meal

Elbow macaroni is ideal for this simple dish but you can use rotini, penne, shells, or whatever smaller pasta you have on hand. Experiment with different types of cheese (sharp, medium, Italian blend, jalapeno cheese) to add some variety to your cooking – all made in a rice cooker!

INGREDIENTS

- **2 cups** uncooked macaroni/pasta
- **2 cups** chicken stock or **2 cups** water
- **1 cup** heavy cream or **1 cup** half-and-half (milk/cream)
- **1 ¼ cups** shredded mixed cheese (mild cheddar, mozzarella, Monterey jack, fontina)
- **2 tbsp** butter
- **¼ tsp** salt and pepper
- **pinch** cayenne pepper
- **1 stick** parsley

HOW TO MAKE

1. Put the macaroni, stock and salt into your rice cooker.

2. Close the lid and press 'WHITE RICE' or 'PASTA' function then press 'START'.

3. When the rice cooker switches to keep warm, add the cream, cheese, cayenne pepper and stir with paddle.

4. Close lid and leave on 'KEEP WARM' until ready to serve. Stays terrific for hours and is best if left for at least 30 minutes on this setting.

5. Serve with a sprinkle of cayenne pepper and parsley on the top for decoration.

   *If larger serving is desired you can double or triple recipe but you may need to add an additional 1/2 cup of liquid if the pasta is not cooked enough,.

HANDY TIP! Easy to store this one in the fridge for a couple of days and reheat when you need it. Try different toppings such as bacon (non veg), panko crumbs or similar to liven it all up.

INDONESIAN CURRY WITH TOFU

A creamy, nutty, spicy vegan curry from the populous nation Indonesia

An amazing vegan dish which is delicious, healthy and really, really easy to cook. One pan is all it takes to create this tasty Indonesian curry. Adding peanut butter at the end gives the curry a lovely rich taste and reminded us of the other famous Indonesian dish, gado-gado.

INGREDIENTS

- **200g** firm tofu, cut into bite sized pieces
- **1 tin (400ml)** coconut milk
- **6 cloves** garlic
- **400g** green beans
- **5** fresh tomatoes and **1** red onion
- **2 tsp** brown sugar or palm sugar
- **2 tsp** peanut butter
- **2 tbsp** soy sauce
- **1 large** red chilli (or more if you like spicy)
- **2-3cm** piece fresh ginger
- **1 tsp** vegetable oil and 100ml water
- **2 rice cooker measuring cups** long grain rice

HOW TO MAKE

1. Chop the onion, garlic, chilli and slice the ginger into thin matchsticks.

2. Heat the oil in a saucepan and add the onion, garlic, chilli and ginger. Cook on low heat for 10 minutes, stir occasionally. If the mixture sticks, add some water.

3. Top and tail the green beans and cut into thirds, roughly chop the tomatoes and add these to the pan.

4. Stir, and cook for another 5 minutes until the tomatoes are softening.

5. Add the coconut milk, water, palm/brown sugar and soy sauce. Cook for a further 20 minutes.

6. Add the tofu and allow to cook for 5 minutes (or longer if you prefer).

7. Stir the peanut butter through the finished curry and add an extra bit of soy sauce or sugar if needed to balance.

8. Serve with long grain rice (brown or white).

   - Optionally add a few peanuts and different vegetables to suit your taste.

HANDY TIP!

This curry goes particularly well with brown rice or a mixture of brown and white rice. We like to use jasmine rice but any long grain rice works.

MINESTRONE SOUP
Thick Italian soup with
small pasta and lots of veg

3   **140"**   **EASY**   **RICE COOKER + PAN**

Although this is technically a meat dish, it can easily be converted to vegetarian/vegan as we have done here. Cooked to perfection using the SOUP/SLOW COOK function of your rice cooker. *For meat eaters you can easily add protein at the end of cooking.

INGREDIENTS

- **small cubes** of vegetables (we use potato, carrot, green beans, baby sweetcorn, red pepper and cauliflower)
- **1** yellow onion
- **1 clove** garlic
- **1 tbsp** tomato puree
- **1 tin** whole plum tomatoes
- **1 vegetable stock cube** and **550ml** hot water
- **3 tbsp** pre-cooked kidney beans
- **3 tbsp** elbow macaroni or other small shaped pasta
- **2 pinches** mixed italian herbs
- **1½ tbsp** sugar (depending on how acidic the tomatoes are)
- **1 pinch** salt and **1 pinch** black pepper
- **1 pinch** paprika
- cornflour mixed with cold water for thickening

HOW TO MAKE

1. Add all the ingredients to your rice cooker and select the 'SOUP' or 'SLOW COOK' function. *Alternatively you can first fry the onions and garlic in a pan with some oil until they are caramelised. Add a splash of water to the pan and a large tablespoon of tomato puree before adding to the rice cooker.

2. Sprinkle some black pepper, coat the onions in the melted tomato puree and add the can of whole plum tomatoes and roughly chop with a spoon.

3. Add hot water (you don't have to use the whole amount if you don't want to), vegetable stock cube, vegetables, sugar, herbs, salt and paprika. Set the cooking time for 2 hours and press 'START' on your rice cooker.

4. After 1 hour, taste and adjust the seasoning, at this point it may need a little more sugar, salt, pepper and paprika. Stir in the kidney beans and elbow macaroni and simmer for another 10 minutes.

5. Thicken the soup with the cornflour and water and continue to cook until the pasta is ready to eat.

6. Once ready, serve into bowls and garnish with vegan parmesan. Serve with a nice warm roll or oatcakes.

HANDY TIP! Use tofu chunks and dipping bread to jazz it up if you feel it's needed. For the meat eaters you can add sliced ham pieces at the serving point to satisfy every craving.

TEAR'N'SHARE PIZZA BREAD

The colours of Italy wrapped up in pizza dough balls to create a pull apart piece of quality snack food

4   **130"**   **MEDIUM**   **RICE COOKER**

Fresh mozzarella, passata and basil wrapped up in simple pizza dough then cooked in a rice cooker makes this very effective tear and share snack.

- **400g** strong (bread or '00') flour
- **15g** dried yeast
- **pinch** salt
- **300ml** warm water (around 45 degrees Celsius)
- **4 tbsp** olive oil

FOR THE FILLING (Marinara sauce)

- **400ml** passata
- **4 cloves** garlic, crushed
- **1 tbsp** mixed herbs
- **1 tbsp** dried oregano
- **handful** fresh basil, chopped
- **pinches** salt, pepper, sugar for seasoning, to taste
- **1 tbsp** plus **1 tsp** olive oil
- **200g** mozzarella cheese in **2cm** squares

HOW TO MAKE

1. **FOR THE DOUGH** - Put the flour in a bowl add the yeast on one side, salt on the other (important these don't touch until liquid is added).

2. Make a well in the centre and add the olive oil. Mix into the flour with a fork and then gradually add the water, mixing with the fork until the dough comes together. If the dough is too wet, add more flour.

3. Tip onto a floured worksurface and knead until smooth (about 5 mins). When formed into a bowl, you can check it's ready by lightly pressing a thumb into the dough, the dough should spring back.

4. Set aside in the bowl (cover with cling film) to proof for 30-60 minutes then once doubled in size, turn out onto a floured work surface and divide into 8 pieces and roll into balls

5. **FOR THE SAUCE** - Put 1 tsp olive oil into a heated pan and gently fry the garlic to release the flavour, make sure it doesn't burn. Turn the heat down and add the passata, herbs, salt, pepper and sugar (you may need ½ a tsp depending on the passata). Cook the sauce on a low heat for 20 minutes and add 1 tbsp olive oil. Set aside to cool.

6. **ASSEMBLY** - Grease the inner bowl of your rice cooker with olive oil. Take a dough ball and flatten on a floured work surface, gently stretching the dough.

7. Place 2 tbsp of sauce on the dough and place a square of mozzarella on top before folding the dough over and sealing the ball.

8. Repeat for all the other dough balls and place into the inner bowl. Gently baste the top of the dough balls with olive oil.

9. Close the lid, select 'CAKE', set time to 50 minutes and press 'START'. When finished carefully tip out onto a plate and place back into the rice cooker so the top can cook further.

10. Select the 'CAKE' function and set for 30 minutes, it will probably be done in 20 minutes. Tip out and serve with the remaining marinara sauce for dipping.

HANDY TIP!

Add black or green olives into the marinara sauce when wrapping for some extra flavour.

Meat eaters could add some ham or prosciutto.

EASY RICE SEASONING MIX RECIPES

Add some spice to your rice!

A very easy way of giving rice a different taste. Making your own seasoning mixes is cheaper than purchasing ready-made mixes. Although purchasing the spices at first costs more, the amount of seasoning mix you can make means it's more economical than buying premade mixes, not to mention they are tastier and healthier with no hidden ingredients. You can add the seasoning to the rice and water or stir through cooked rice.

PIRI PIRI SEASONING MIX

Stir all ingredients together until combined well.
- **2 tbsp** sugar
- **2 tbsp** paprika
- **2 tbsp** onion powder
- **2 tbsp** garlic powder
- **2 tbsp** ground coriander
- **1 tbsp** salt
- **1 tbsp** dried oregano
- **1 tbsp** dried parsley
- **2 tsp** ground ginger
- **2 tsp** ground cardamon
- **1 tsp** smoked paprika
- **1 tsp** cayenne pepper

MOROCCAN (Ras-El-Hanout) MIX

Stir all ingredients together until combined well.
- **1 tsp** ground cumin
- **1 tsp** ground ginger
- **1 tsp** salt
- **¾ tsp** black pepper
- **½ tsp** ground cinnamon
- **½ tsp** ground coriander
- **½ tsp** cayenne
- **½ tsp** ground allspice
- **¼ tsp** ground cloves

CAJUN SEASONING MIX

Stir all ingredients together until combined well.
- **2 tsp** salt
- **2 tsp** garlic powder
- **2 ½ tsp** paprika
- **1 tsp** ground black pepper
- **1 tsp** onion powder
- **1 tsp** cayenne pepper
- **1 ¼ tsp** dried oregano
- **1 ¼ tsp** dried thyme
- **½ tsp** red chilli flakes (optional)

SPANISH RICE SEASONING MIX

- **1 tbsp** dried onion
- **3 tbsp** dried red chilli flakes (or less to taste)
- **1 tbsp** dried celery flakes
- **1 tsp** chicken bouillon granules
- **½ tsp** salt
- **¼ tsp** garlic powder

INDIAN CURRY SEASONING MIX

Add all spices to a small jar and shake.
- **2 tbsp** ground coriander
- **2 tbsp** ground cumin
- **1½ tbsp** ground turmeric
- **2 tsp** ground ginger
- **1 tsp** dry mustard
- **½ tsp** ground black pepper
- **1 tsp** ground cinnamon
- **½ tsp** ground cardamom
- **½ tsp** cayenne pepper or ground chilies

CORIANDER LIME MIX

Add to rice after cooking
- **½ whole** lime (juiced)
- **1 tsp** salt
- **3 tbsp** fresh chopped coriander

BAHARAT SEASONING MIX

(Baharat (which means 'spices' in Arabic) is a spice blend used in Middle Eastern (especially the Arabian Gulf region) and Greek cuisine. **Stir all ingredients together until combined well.**
- **1 tbsp** ground black pepper
- **2 tsp** ground nutmeg
- **2 tsp** paprika
- **1 tsp** ground coriander
- **1 tsp** ground cinnamon
- **1 tsp** ground cloves
- **1 tsp** ground cumin
- **1 tsp** salt
- **¼ tsp** ground cardamom
- **½ tsp** cayenne pepper or ground chilies

PANDA'S SIMPLE SEASONING MIX

- **½ cup** chicken bouillon granules
- **½ cup** dried parsley flakes
- **1 tbsp** dried basil
- **1 tbsp** dill
- **1 tbsp** dried onion
- **1 tbsp** salt
- **1 tsp** garlic powder
- **1 tsp** lemon-pepper seasoning

JAMAICAN JERK SEASONING MIX

Stir all ingredients together until combined well.
- **1 tbsp** onion powder
- **1 tbsp** garlic powder
- **2 tsp** cayenne pepper
- **2 tsp** smoked paprika (regular paprika is fine)
- **1 tsp** ground allspice
- **2 tsp** salt
- **1 tsp** black pepper ground
- **½ tsp** red pepper flakes
- **½ tsp** cumin ground
- **½ tsp** nutmeg ground
- **½ tsp** cinnamon ground
- **1 tbsp** brown sugar
- **1 tsp** thyme dried
- **1 tbsp** parsley dried

MEAT

ROGAN JOSH WITH BASMATI RICE

Worth the effort for an authentic taste of India

2/3   95"   HARD   RICE COOKER + PAN

Traditionally made with lamb or mutton, it can also be made with chicken or beef. Ideal for rice cooker preparation using the slow cook and basmati cooking functions. It's also a favourite of our greedy panda!

● INGREDIENTS FOR THE PASTE

2 cloves garlic
2-3cm piece fresh root ginger (or 1 tsp of minced ginger from a jar)
¼ cup roasted peppers, from a jar
1 tbsp paprika
1 tsp smoked paprika
2 tsp garam masala
1 tsp turmeric
½ tsp sea salt
2 tbsp groundnut oil (sunflower oil works too)
2 tbsp tomato purée
2 fresh red chillies (we used birds eye chilli with the seeds in)
½ cup fresh coriander
2 tsp cumin seeds
2 tsp coriander seeds
1 tsp black peppercorns

● INGREDIENTS FOR THE CURRY

500g of your preferred meat (lamb, mutton, beef or chicken) cut into large chunks
1 large onion (red or yellow) chopped into chunks
500ml tomato passata
200ml milk (any type cow/soy/oat/almond)
3 pinches salt, pepper, sugar
1 dash vegetable oil
1 stick fresh coriander (for garnish)

2 rice measuring cups white basmati rice to serve on the side (enough for 2-3 people)

HOW TO MAKE

1. Combine the paste ingredients into a food processor and blend so it forms a paste. You may need to add more oil if the mixture is too dry. Just add a little more at a time until the paste loosens.

2. Heat the oil in a saucepan. When it's nice and hot you can add the chopped onions and cook for 5 minutes.

3. Add the meat to the onions and seal. Once sealed, add the curry paste with a splash of water to loosen the paste. Stir and make sure the meat and onion is well coated in the paste.

4. Add the passata to the pan, season with salt, pepper and around 2 tsp sugar (taste first, will depend on the passata).

5. Stir to ensure all ingredients are combined. Add the milk little by little until the consistency of the sauce is thick, but still a bit loose.

6. Transfer to your rice cooker bowl and then select the 'SLOW COOK' function. Set for 2 hours if cooking chicken, or 4 hours for lamb, mutton or beef and press 'START'.

7. Put the basmati rice into your rice cooker, select 'LONG GRAIN' or 'WHITE RICE' and press 'START'

8. Check the seasoning of the curry is correct. If the curry is too spicy, add some more milk; if it's not spicy enough add some dried chilli powder.

9. Serve with fresh coriander sprinkled on top next to a bowl of hot basmati rice.

HANDY TIP! Bulk prepare the paste and store in an airtight jar in the fridge until you are ready to use it. This way you can speed up preparation of this meal for another time.

SPICY CHICKEN SATAY

Great as a snack that's easy, quick and filling

An easy but clever way to impress, this popular dish is made from small pieces of meat or fish grilled on a skewer and served with a spicy peanut sauce. Originating from Indonesia and Malaysia it also goes well with rice.

2	60"	EASY	RICE COOKER + PAN

INGREDIENTS FOR MARINADE

¼ **tsp** turmeric
2 cloves finely chopped garlic
1 stick finely chopped lemongrass
1 tbsp light soy sauce
1 tbsp fish sauce
1 tbsp palm sugar
splash dark soy sauce

FOR THE PASTE

5 Thai shallots, finely diced
1 large red chilli
2 cloves garlic
1 stick lemongrass

FOR THE SAUCE

6 tbsp crunchy peanut butter
2 tbsp tamarind concentrate
2 tbsp kecap manis (sweet soy sauce)
1 tbsp palm sugar
¼ **tsp** salt
100ml hot water

HOW TO MAKE

1. Place bamboo skewers in a dish of cold water. Set them aside and soak for 1 hour.

2. Slice the chicken thighs into long slices. Mix all of the marinade ingredients in a bowl and add the sliced chicken.

3. Massage the marinade mix into the meat. Skewer the chicken and put aside.

4. Blend the paste ingredients to a smooth paste then fry the paste in a saucepan along with 1-2 tbsp vegetable oil for 5 minutes until fragrant and a little brown.

5. In another bowl mix all of the sauce ingredients together. Pour the mixture into the saucepan with the paste and bring to a simmer. Reduce the contents by half. This is your satay sauce which you can now pour into a serving bowl.

6. Heat up a frying pan to high. Splash in some vegetable oil, then place your chicken skewers into the pan and cook on one side for 3-4 minutes. Turn and do the same to the other side, making sure that the chicken is golden brown in colour and has a plentiful char on both sides.

7. Serve on a plate, accompanied by the satay sauce and yes, once again, this goes great with rice!

Get dipping!

HANDY TIP!

For vegans the satay goes well with tofu or even vegan meat substitute.

It's important to allow the char to develop on the chicken when cooking to bring out the best flavour.

CHILLI CON CARNE WITH RICE

Arguably the most popular
and worldly Tex-Mex
dish with rice

 4-6   200"   HARD    RICE COOKER + PAN

We love our chilli con carne, a perfect mix of savoury, meaty and tomato flavour. It's a bit more complicated with several ingredients compared to our other recipes but it makes at least 4 good portions so you can freeze individual portions for another time. Trust us - it's well worth the effort!

INGREDIENTS

- **1kg** minced beef
- **800ml** passata sauce and tomato purée
- **3** jalapeno chillies (either fresh or tin/jar) chop finely – we use 4 for extra spicy!
- **1 small** red pepper – diced very finely
- **2 cloves** garlic, crushed, **2 beef stock cubes**
- **1** yellow or red onion – finely chopped
- **1 tin (400ml)** kidney beans, rinsed and drained
- **1 tsp** cumin powder
- **(optional) 2 squares** dark chocolate (70% or similar)
- **1 tsp** smoked paprika
- **¼ tsp** cayenne pepper
- **2 sticks** coriander fresh
- **1 tsp** chipotle paste, salt/pepper to taste
- **4-6 rice measuring cups** long grain rice

HOW TO MAKE

1. In a pan, fry onions, red pepper and jalapenos in a little oil. When the onions are starting to brown add the beef.

2. Once the beef is sealed, add garlic, stock cubes and cook for 3-4mins. Add the passata, purée, spices, chipotle paste and combine all ingredients by stirring thoroughly.

3. Add the kidney beans to the sauce along with the chocolate and stir to combine. Check the seasoning and adjust if necessary. If the sauce is thick, add a little water and if it's not quite spicy enough you can add a pinch of chilli powder.

4. Transfer the mixture to your rice cooker and select the 'SLOW COOK' function, press 'START' and cook for at least 3 hours.

5. Serve with rice and nacho tortilla chips. Yummy and very filling, so make sure you are hungry!

HANDY TIP! Our top tip – adding a couple of squares of dark chocolate to your chilli makes the flavours deeper and adds a lovely richness to the sauce.

KIMCHI SPECIAL FRIED RICE

SPICY

What's so special? It has an egg on top of course!

🍴 4   🕐 60"   👨‍🍳 EASY   🍚 RICE COOKER + PAN

Kimchi is a Korean fermented dish that often uses red pepper powder, shrimp paste, and/or garlic for flavouring. Like a spicy and sour pickle, adding it to fried rice not only makes it flavourful but also vibrant in colour!

INGREDIENTS

- **3 rice measuring cups** short grain rice (or medium grain rice)
- **1 cup** well fermented kimchi, cut into thumbnail size pieces
- **150g** bacon, cut into thumbnail size pieces
- **4 large** eggs cooked sunny side up
- **½ tsp** minced garlic
- **¼ cup** kimchi juice (the more fermented the better) – this liquid is from the bottom of the kimchi container
- **½ tbsp** sesame oil
- **1 tbsp** cooking oil
- **1 tbsp** toasted sesame seeds to garnish
- **½ stalk** spring onion to garnish, thinly sliced (optional)
- Roasted seasoned seaweed, shredded

HOW TO MAKE

1. Put the rice into your rice cooker bowl and fill to the level 3 white/short grain rice line with water.

2. Press 'WHITE' or 'SHORT GRAIN' function and then 'START'. Leave to cool for 30 minutes after cooking.

3. Heat a pan/wok on medium heat, add the cooking oil.

4. Add the garlic, stir fast for 10 seconds then add the bacon and stir until it's half cooked.

5. Add the kimchi and stir until it's 80% cooked.

6. Reduce the heat to low then add the rice and kimchi juice. Mix together. In a separate pan, fry the eggs.

7. Add the sesame oil to the rice and mix. Remove from the heat.

8. Serve and garnish with the sesame seeds, spring onion and seaweed strips (garnish is all optional).

9. Serve the rice and place the cooked egg on top.

HANDY TIP!
Ideally kimchi is at least 2 weeks old. If not, add ⅓ tsp rice vinegar into the kimchi juice to make it sour. Obtaining ¼ cup of kimchi juice can be difficult if your kimchi is fairly new. In that case, use 2½ tbsp kimchi juice and 1 tbsp gochujang paste

4   70"   **MEDIUM**   **RICE COOKER + PAN**

PUMPKIN WITH CHICKEN CURRY

This fusion recipe mixes Caribbean freshness and central Asian mild spiciness

A fusion of three cuisine types merges together in this recipe. We mix south Asia with Moroccan and Caribbean blends to give a fresh flavourful pumpkin meat hit.

● INGREDIENTS

8 bone-in chicken thighs
1 whole lime juice
pinches sea salt and black pepper

● FOR THE MARINADE

4 spring onions, chopped
4 cloves, garlic chopped
20g fresh root ginger, peeled and chopped
2 scotch bonnets, seeded and finely chopped
zest and juice of 1 lime
2 tbsp medium curry blend - ideally Caribbean
½ tsp ground allspice

● FOR THE CURRY

1 tbsp vegetable oil
1 onion, thickly sliced
300ml chicken stock
2 tomatoes, peeled and diced
2 large thyme sprigs
2 bay leaves
400g pumpkin, cut into large chunks
Juice of ½ lime
1 tsp rum (optional)

HOW TO MAKE

1. Skin the chicken, season with salt/pepper. Put the marinade ingredients into food processor and blend to a paste – add water if needed.

2. Pour the marinade over the chicken. Mix thoroughly to make sure the chicken is fully covered. Cover and leave for a couple of hours (overnight in fridge is best).

3. For the curry, heat the oil in a large casserole dish. Add the onion and cook it over a medium heat for several minutes until it starts to turn golden-brown. Add chicken and marinade to the dish – the idea is not to brown the chicken but to cook the marinade. Add the stock (water is fine if you don't have stock).

4. Add tomatoes, thyme and bay leaves and season with salt/pepper. Bring to a boil, then reduce the heat, cover and simmer for 40 minutes. You can cook in the rice cooker on the 'SLOW COOK' setting for 1 hour if preferred

5. Add the pumpkin and cook for a further 10 minutes, covered. Pour in the lime juice and the rum, if using. Remove the lid and cook for another 5–10 minutes to reduce the sauce slightly and finish off cooking the pumpkin.

6. Serve with steamed white rice or cous cous for balance. Top with spring onions or coriander.

HANDY TIP! Add grated coconut cream at the end or 100ml of coconut milk with the stock to give it a more coconut flavour. If you want less heat use 1 less Scotch bonnet.

MASSAMAN CURRY WITH JASMINE RICE

Great for both summer and winter!

2 **80"** **HARD** **RICE COOKER + PAN**

Massaman curry or kaeng matsaman is a delicious Thai curry which has a very distinct spicy but not (chilli) hot taste. One of our favourite Thai curries and worth persevering despite the more complex preparation.

● INGREDIENTS FOR THE PASTE

- **5** shallots, unpeeled
- **2 cloves** garlic, unpeeled
- **2 tbsp** sliced galangal
- **1 stick** lemongrass, sliced
- **1 tbsp** coriander seeds
- **1 tsp** cumin seeds
- **2** cloves
- **1 tsp** peppercorns
- **3** dried red spur chillies, deseeded and soaked until tender
- **1 tsp** sea salt
- **1 tsp** ground cardamom
- **1 tsp** shrimp paste

● INGREDIENTS FOR THE CURRY

- **½ tsp** cumin seeds
- **5** cardamom pods
- **5** cloves
- **1 small** cinnamon stick or **¼ tsp** ground cinnamon
- **2 tbsp** vegetable oil
- **2 generous tbsp** Massaman curry paste (see above)
- **3** bay leaves
- **1 medium** onion, roughly chopped
- **300–400ml** (1 tin) of coconut milk
- **2 tbsp** palm sugar and **1 tsp** caster sugar
- **2 tbsp** Thai fish sauce
- **2 tbsp** tamarind paste
- **1** potato, peeled and cut into bite-sized pieces
- **200g** beef sirloin, cut into bite-sized pieces
- **2 tbsp** beef or vegetable stock (optional)
- **2 tbsp** roasted cashew nuts
- **5 pieces** pineapple chunks
- **pinch** sea salt

HOW TO MAKE

1. For the paste use a wok or frying pan to dry-fry the whole shallots and garlic for 5-10 minutes until golden and soft. Set aside to cool, then peel off the skin.

2. Dry-fry the galangal and lemongrass using a medium heat until fragrant and slightly golden, about 2–3 minutes. Set aside.

3. Dry-fry the coriander seeds, cumin, cloves and peppercorns for 2 minutes until fragrant, stirring continuously.

4. Put the above ingredients in a mortar and pestle and pound (or use a food processor). Finely pound the chillies and salt and add the roasted galangal and lemongrass and keep pounding well.

5. Add the shallots and garlic and continue to pound/blend, then add the ground roasted spices, the cardamom and the shrimp paste. Mix until smooth.

6. Heat the oil in a large heavy-based pan or a wok over medium-low heat. Add the onion and cook for 5 minutes.

7. Add massaman paste and cook for 1 minute or until fragrant. Add the beef and cook, stirring, for 3 minutes or until browned. Add the garlic and ginger and cook for 1 minute.

8. Add coconut milk, stock, cinnamon, chilli, bay leaves, palm sugar, fish sauce, peanuts and potato to the pan and bring to the boil. Reduce heat to low. Cover and simmer until the beef is very tender.

9. Serve with jasmine rice.

HANDY TIP! This curry works best with chicken, beef or tofu. Garnish with a few peanuts (careful of allergies). Brown jasmine or a 2:1 mix of white jasmine to riecberry rice also pairs well.

-38-

HUNGARIAN BEEF GOULASH

Time to put that slow cooker function on your rice cooker to work!

4-6 | **70"** | **MEDIUM** | **RICE COOKER + PAN**

Tender beef with a flavourful kick from central Europe. Perfect for a cool evening or hearty filling meal. Serve with rice, noodles, good quality bread (for sauce dunking) or a home made creamy mash for a winning combination.

INGREDIENTS

- **1kg** good braising steak, ideally chuck steak (trim hard fat, cut into 4cm chunks)

- **400g (tin)** chopped tomatoes

- **2 tbsp** tomato purée

- **3** medium onions, cut into wedges (we use red onions)

- **3** garlic cloves, crushed

- **2** red peppers

- **1** orange pepper

- **2 tsp** smoked paprika

- **1 tbsp** sweet paprika

- **2** bay leaves

- **2** beef stock cubes (we use Oxo)

- **1 tbsp** sunflower or olive oil

- **600ml** cold water

- **pinches** salt and ground black pepper

HOW TO MAKE

1. Season the steak well with salt and black pepper. Heat the oil in a large pan, add the steak and fry over a high heat until nicely browned all over, turning regularly.

2. Add the onions and cook with the beef for around 5 minutes. Add the crushed garlic and cook for another minute.

3. Sprinkle the paprikas over the meat and crumble the beef stock cube on top. Add the water (bit by bit to get to the consistency you like), tomatoes, tomato purée and bay leaves. Season with salt and pepper, stir well and bring to a simmer.

4. Transfer to the rice cooker and select the 'SLOW COOK' function on your rice cooker. Press 'START' We suggest a minimum of 2 hours but you can adjust to your taste.

5. Cut each pepper into big chunks and add to the cooker bowl and cook for 10 minutes.

HANDY TIP! After seasoning you can coat the beef in plain flour to help tenderise it and will also have the effect of thickening the sauce

THAI CHILLI BASIL CHICKEN WITH JASMINE RICE

Ideal for quick lunches with a fiery kick

A tasty but simple Thai dish – this is a 'go-to' meal all over Thailand for lunch, it's usually served 'on rice' and topped with a fried egg hat.We prefer our eggs semi runny and is the normal serving style.

2   **55"**   **EASY**   **RICE COOKER + PAN**

INGREDIENTS

- **1** chicken breast diced into small pieces
- **10** green beans diced (small pieces)
- **4** crushed garlic cloves
- **4** birds eye chillies de-seeded and finely chopped (this is very spicy, add less if you like it milder or leave the seed in if you like spicy!)
- **5 pinches** basil leaves (can be Thai holy basil or regular basil)
- **4 tbsp** soy sauce
- **¼ tsp** sugar
- **4 tbsp** water (add cornflour to thicken if necessary)
- **2 rice measuring cups** white jasmine rice

HOW TO MAKE

1. Put the rice into your rice cooker bowl and fill to the level 2 white rice line (for 2 rice cups) with water.

2. Press the 'WHITE', 'REGULAR' or 'LONG GRAIN' function and then 'START'.

3. In a pan, stir fry garlic, onions and chilli to release flavour then add chicken and green beans. Stir fry until the chicken is cooked.

4. Add 4 tbsp of soy sauce, 0.5 -2 tsp of sugar (depending on taste) and as much water as you need for it to taste ok for your spice tolerance.

5. Thicken with a little cornflour mixed with water and simmer for 5-10 minutes.

6. Add the basil leaves and cook for a further 2-4 minutes until basil leaves are wilted.

7. Adjust seasoning, adding more soy sauce and sugar if needed.

8. Serve with jasmine rice on the side.

HANDY TIP! The egg on the top is a very popular way of way of serving this dish in Thailand. It may seem strange at first but try it and you will be amazed at how the flavours become perfectly balanced.
For vegans, remove the egg and chicken and use tofu or plant based mince instead.

FIERY MAPO TOFU

Sichuan peppercorns and ground meat with a tofu base

2/3   **85"**   **HARD**   **RICE COOKER + PAN**

This popular Chinese dish from Sichuan province consists of tofu set in a spicy sauce, typically a thin, oily, and bright red suspension, based on douban and douchi pastes, along with minced meat, traditionally beef or pork.

● INGREDIENTS

6-10 dry red chillies (soaked in hot water)
1 small onion
2 cloves garlic
2 fresh bird's-eye chillies
small handful of coriander
300g firm silken tofu (fresh or packaged tofu are both good)
2 tsp preserved black beans
1 tsp Sichuan peppercorns
200g pork mince or beef mince
2 tbsp oil
2 rice measuring cups long grain white rice (or brown)

● FOR THE MARINADE

1 tsp sesame oil
pinch granulated sugar
1 tbsp light soy sauce

● FOR THE SAUCE

2 tsp chilli bean paste or hot chilli paste
2 tbsp light soy sauce
3 tbsp rice wine
1 tbsp Gochujang Korean pepper paste
400ml chicken stock

FOR THE CORNFLOUR PASTE
2 tsp cornflour
3 tbsp water

HOW TO MAKE

1. Dice the onion. Finely chop the garlic, bird's-eye chillies and coriander. Cut the silken tofu into 2cm cubes.

2. Wash and drain the preserved black beans, place them in a sealable plastic bag with the Sichuan peppercorns and bash with a rolling pin until lightly crushed.

3. Place the meat in a bowl, add the marinade ingredients and massage together well with your hands. Mix the sauce ingredients together in a separate bowl.

4. Add 2 cups of rice to your rice cooker bowl at this point and fill to the white rice level 2 line. Use the 'WHITE RICE', 'LONG GRAIN' or 'REGULAR' function on your rice cooker and press 'START'

5. Heat the oil in a wok over a medium-high heat until smoking-hot then add the onion. Stir-fry for 1 minute until the onions are lightly browned and starting to soften.

6. Add the garlic, black bean and peppercorn mix and chilli to the pan, followed immediately by the marinated pork. Stir-fry for a further 2 minutes, until the pork/beef mince is separated and browned, then pour over the sauce and bring to a vigorous boil.

7. Add cornflour paste gradually until you get the desired thickness of the sauce then add the diced tofu to the wok, reduce the heat to medium and simmer for 5 minutes, stirring gently so as not to break up the tofu pieces. Continue to bubble away until the sauce has thickened and reduced by a third, but the dish is still nice and brothy.

8. Serve with rice in a large bowl and scatter over the finely chopped coriander togarnish.

HANDY TIP! Adjust the spice on this one by carefully using less or more chillies and peppercorns. Obviously less will reduce the heat but try it spicy and use the rice to cool the mouth

3/4   **70"**   **EASY**   **RICE COOKER + PAN**

CHICKEN KORMA WITH BASMATI RICE

A rich, creamy authentic Indian party dish

An authentic Indian korma, rich and ideal for entertaining. Not spicy but certainly one of the more flavourful creamy dishes that works well with rice..

INGREDIENTS

- **2** chicken breasts, diced into 2cm pieces
- **¼ tsp** chilli powder and **1 tsp** turmeric
- **1 heaped tbsp** garam masala
- **4 tbsp** natural yoghurt or creme fraiche
- **2-3 tsp** brown sugar and **⅓ tsp** salt to taste
- **2 heaped tbsp** ground almonds
- **1 handful** coriander (chopped finely)
- **1 tbsp** pomegranate seeds
- **2 tbsp** vegetable oil
- **1 tsp** cumin seeds
- **1 large** or **2 small** white onion diced finely
- **5cm** ginger peeled and grated
- **2 cloves** garlic crushed
- **2 rice measuring cups** basmati rice

HOW TO MAKE

1. Put 2 rice measuring cups of basmati rice into the rice cooker bowl and fill with water to the level 2 line for white/long grain rice. Select the 'WHITE', 'REGULAR' or 'LONG GRAIN' function on your rice cooker and press 'START'.

2. Add the oil to a wok or pan, then add and brown the onion, ginger and garlic.

3. Add the chicken breast and cook for a few minutes on a medium heat until it colours.

4. Add the turmeric, chilli, and the garam masala.

5. Stir-fry for a minute.

6. Add the yoghurt or creme fraiche and a touch of water to loosen the sauce.

7. Simmer for around 7 minutes until the chicken is cooked then add the salt, sugar and ground almonds.

8. Give it a good stir and serve with the rice, garnished with the coriander and pomegranate seeds.

HANDY TIP!

If you like your curry spicy then simply add some chopped fresh chillies.

Garnish with coriander, some almonds or pomegranate seeds.

GREEN CHICKEN CURRY WITH JASMINE RICE

Vibrant spicy goodness from the Thai South

SPICY

4 | **110"** | **HARD** | **RICE COOKER + PAN**

This green curry is one of the most famous and warming Thai dishes. It's green colour is derived from green chillies, introduced to Thailand by early Portuguese traders, coriander, turmeric and makrut (kaffir lime) leaves. The dish is said to be from the early 20th century but could be much older.

INGREDIENTS FOR CURRY PASTE

750g large green chillies
6g cumin seeds (ground and toasted)
4g coriander seeds (ground and toasted)
6g black peppercorns (ground and toasted)
30g fresh galangal root (chopped)
50g lemongrass (chopped)
70g fresh turmeric
70g garlic (chopped)
15g makrut lime (Kaffir) zest
130g chopped shallots
20g small hot green chillies

INGREDIENTS FOR CURRY

200g curry paste made with the above ingredients
60g vegetable oil
500g coconut milk
500g chicken sliced into strips
100g green beans
3 makrut lime leaves (Kaffir)
50g palm sugar
250g chicken stock
45g fish sauce
2g salt
4 Thai aubergines cut into quarters
100g pea aubergines (stems removed)
5 sticks of Thai holy basil
5 red bird's eye chillies
Serve with **4 rice measuring cups** jasmine rice

HOW TO MAKE

1. Make the paste by combining the paste ingredients using a hand blender or stone mortar and pestle, if you want a workout.

2. Fry the makrut leaves in hot oil (don't burn them) then add the curry paste whilst stirring briskly until the fragrance is released (about 2 minutes).

3. Pour in half of the coconut milk and keep stirring so it doesn't burn.

4. Reduce the sauce by one third and when the oil forms on top, turn up to a high heat

5. Season to taste with salt, palm sugar, chicken stock and the remaining coconut milk. Bring to a boil.

6. Add the chicken and cook for 5 minutes before adding the rest of the vegetables.

7. Cook for a 4-5 more minutes then add fish sauce and garnish with basil leaves and red chillies.

8. Serve with jasmine rice cooked in your rice cooker.

HANDY TIP! Make the curry paste in advance to save time. Make in a well ventilated kitchen as it can be very potent. Use rice to balance the heat!

GREEK CHICKEN WITH LEMON RICE

Tender chicken against the star of the dish, fresh lemon flavour

2-4 | 90" | EASY | RICE COOKER

Not neccessarily authentic Greek but this dish has ingredients typical from that part of the Meditteranean. All done in a rice cooker this recipe is only tricky to get the right liquid to rice ratios, which a rice cooker can help with.

● INGREDIENTS FOR CHICKEN

5 chicken thighs, skin on, bone in (about 1 kg)*
1 - 2 lemons, use the zest + 4 tbsp lemon juice**
1 tbsp dried oregano
4 cloves garlic, minced
½ tsp salt

● FOR THE RICE

1 ½ tbsp olive oil, separated
1 small onion, finely diced
1 cup (180g) long grain rice , uncooked***
1 ½ cups (375ml) chicken broth/stock
¾ cup (185ml) water
2 fresh tomaties, sliced
1 tbsp dried oregano
¾ tsp salt
pinch black pepper
finely chopped parsley or oregano (optional)
fresh lemon zest (highly recommended)

HOW TO MAKE

1. Combine the chicken and marinade ingredients in a ziplock bag and set aside for at least 20 minutes but preferably overnight. Remove chicken from marinade, but reserve the marinade.

2. Press 'SLOW COOK' on your rice cooker and add 1 tbsp oil. Place the chicken in the inner bowl cook until golden brown, then turn and cook the other side until golden brown. Remove the chicken and set aside. Pour away the oil and lightly wipe the bowl.

3. Heat 1 tbsp olive oil in the inner bowl and add the onion and sauté for a few minutes until translucent. Then add the remaining rice ingredients and reserved marinade, stir to combine. Cancel the 'SLOW COOK' setting and select 'WHITE RICE', 'REGULAR' or 'LONG GRAIN' function and press 'START'.

4. When the rice is finished (usually around 30-40 minutes) add the chicken to the top of the cooked rice along with the sliced tomatoes.

5. Press 'SLOW COOK' once again and cook for around 15-20 minutes until the chicken is cooked through.

6. Fluff rice to loosen, taste and add salt and pepper if needed. Squeeze fresh lemon juice over chicken and rice, and serve.

HANDY TIP! For a fresher taste you can add some sliced lemons (saute if you prefer) to the top of the dish when slow cooking at the end. Sprinkle some fresh parsley over the top to garnish.

CHINESE BEEF AND TOMATO

A fakeaway faster than ordering a takeaway and just as tasty

2/3 **75"** **MEDIUM** **RICE COOKER + PAN**

You won't be craving your Chinese takeaway so much after trying this recipe! Don't be put off by the 3 separate ingredient lists for this recipe, it's actually not as difficult as you may think.

● FOR THE BEEF MARINADE

500g beef or steak sliced into thin pieces
1 tbsp cornflour
1 tsp vegetable oil
¼ tsp salt

● FOR THE SAUCE BASE

2 tbsp tomato ketchup
2 tbsp light soy sauce
1½ tsp sugar
½ tsp sesame oil
pinch freshly ground white pepper to taste

● FOR THE REST OF THE DISH

3 tbsp vegetable oil
3 sticks thinly sliced ginger
1 clove garlic, finely minced
¼ cup sliced shallot (or red onion)
1 large spring onion, cut into 2-inch pieces at an angle
4 large tomatoes, cut into wedges
1 tbsp Shaoxing wine
½ tbsp cornfour mixed with 1 tbsp water
2-3 rice measuring cups jasmine rice or similar long grain

HANDY TIP! The marinade is important as it helps to tenderise the beef. Do this for one hour minimum, 3 hours is better.

HOW TO MAKE

1. Marinate the meat with the cornflour, salt and the first teaspoon of oil. Set aside for one hour. Combine all the ingredients for the sauce base in a separate bowl.

2. Put the rice into your rice cooker inner bowl, add water to the corresponding level line, select the rice function for the rice you are cooking. Press 'START'.

3. Add 1 tbsp of oil to coat the wok and heat until just smoking. Spread the beef around the wok and sear for 1 minute until 80% done, remove from the wok and set aside.

4. Heat 1 tbsp of oil in the wok over medium heat. Add the ginger slices, and let them caramelise for 10 seconds.

5. Turn the heat up to high and add the minced garlic, shallot/red onion and the white portions of the spring onion. Toss and cook for 10 seconds.

6. Add the tomato wedges to the wok and spread around to sear for around 15 seconds. Add the Shaoxing wine, stir-fry the mixture for another 10 seconds until the alcohol has burned off. Push everything to one side of the wok.

7. In a cleared area of the wok, add the sauce base. Stir until bubbling to combine the flavours together.

8. Add the beef and any juices in the bowl back into the wok. Stir-fry everything on high heat until mixed well and sizzling (only takes about 20 seconds). Make sure you don't overcook the tomatoes or they will completely disintegrate into the sauce!

9. Add the remainder of the spring onion and add the cornflour/water mix a little at a time until sauce is thickened to your liking.

10. Serve with your rice!

GYUDON (Japanese Beef Bowl)

Synonymous with comfort, this 150 year old dish is yum!

2-3   **50"**   **EASY**   **RICE COOKER + PAN**

Gyudon is classic comfort food that has had its place in Japanese cuisine for over 150 years. It's a hearty rice bowl that is very simple to put together. While every household in Japan makes it a little different, the core ingredients remain the same: thin slices of beef, onion, egg, and a sweet and savoury sauce served over a bed of hot rice.

INGREDIENTS

- **2 rice measuring cups** Japanese short grain rice (approx 360ml rice)
- **340g** thinly sliced beef (chuck or rib eye)
- **110g** onion
- **2** spring onions/scallions
- **1 tbsp** neutral-flavored oil (vegetable, rice bran, canola, etc)
- **3 large** eggs (beaten optional)
- **3 tbsp** soy sauce
- **1 tbsp** sugar
- **2 tbsp** mirin
- **2 tbsp** sake (substitute with dry sherry or Chinese rice wine; for a non-alcoholic sub, use water)

HOW TO MAKE

1. Add rice to the rice cooker bowl. Fill with water to the short grain level 2. Select the 'SHORT GRAIN' function and press 'START'.

2. Thinly slice the onions, cut the spring onions into thin slices (save for garnish) and cut the meat into thin 7cm slices.

3. Heat the oil in a large frying pan over a medium heat and cook the onion until tender (about 3-5 minutes).

4. Add the meat and sugar to the pan, and cook until meat is no longer pink.

5. Add sake, mirin, and soy sauce and reduce the heat and simmer for 3-5 minutes.

6. Slowly drizzle the beaten egg over the beef. Cook with a lid on until the egg is almost done (don't overcook it).

7. In a medium bowl (donburi) add steamed rice and put the beef and egg mixture on top. Drizzle over the remaining sauce (optional).

HANDY TIP!
Top with green onion and pickled red ginger (beni shoga or kizami beni shoga) to garnish.

INDIAN NARIYAL CHICKEN CURRY

A hybrid curry, with a Northern Indian spice base and the creamy coconut of Southern Indian curries

4   **70"**   **HARD**   **RICE COOKER + PAN**

Made with chicken and typical South Indian ingredients like coconut milk and curry leaves, this creamy spicy dish tastes best with rice. Serve it for a family meal and portion it up for tasty lunches.

● FOR THE RICE

4 rice measuring cups basmati white rice

● INGREDIENTS FOR THE CURRY

2 chicken thighs or breast, trimmed and cut into bite size chunks

1 potato cut into small pieces (pre-boil these for 5 minutes to partially cook), carrots sliced, green beans, broccoli, bell pepper.

1 tbsp coconut or vegetable oil

1 tsp cumin seeds (or cumin powder)

2 medium onions, blended in a food processor to a grated consistency

400ml tin plum tomatoes

1 tsp salt with **1 tsp** turmeric

½ tsp chilli powder (optional)

2 green or red chillies, chopped (if you want it spicy, leave the seeds in)

1 tin coconut cream or milk

1 tsp garam masala

10 pinches fresh coriander, chopped

HOW TO MAKE

1. Add 4 rice measuring cups of basmati rice to your rice cooker inner bowl, then fill to the level 4 white rice level line with water. Select the 'WHITE RICE' or 'REGULAR' function and press 'START'.

2. Heat the oil in a pan, then add cumin seeds/powder. When sizzling and aromatic add the onions and fry until they are golden.

3. Add the tin of tomatoes, salt, turmeric and fresh chillies.

4. Stir together and leave to cook so the tomatoes break down and you're left with a very thick paste.

5. Pour in the coconut cream/milk and cook gently for a few minutes so the flavours combine.

6. Add the meat and vegetables to the pan and stir to coat with the sauce.

7. Reduce the heat to the lowest setting and place the lid half on the pan and leave to simmer for about 20 minutes, make sure the potatoes are cooked, if not, cook for a little longer

8. Taste the sauce and adjust seasoning if required and add the chilli powder if you need to.

9. Remove from the heat and add garam masala and throw in the fresh coriander. Serve with rice.

HANDY TIP! This curry can easily be adapted to vegetarian or vegan, just replace the meat with your favourite pulses, add sweet potato. Spinach would also be really good in this curry.

-47-

CHICKEN DO PYAZA

Aromatic chicken and onion curry
inspired by Mughal and Persian cuisines

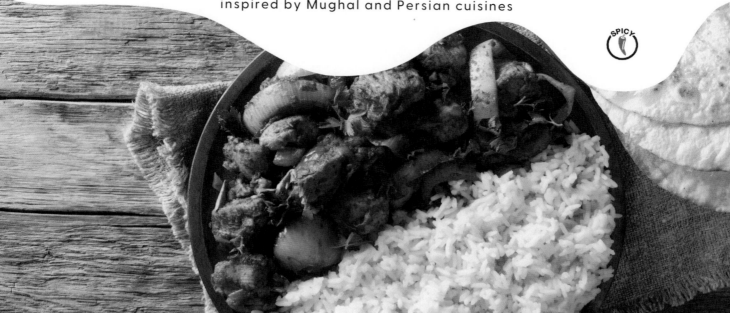

4   **80"**   **HARD**   **RICE COOKER + PAN**

In India, do (pronounced 'dough'), means two and pyaza is onion. Do pyaza refers to the onions being used in two ways. Diced onions are first fried with spices and then larger pieces of onions are added at the end to give a spicy dish which is also sweet from the onions. The pyaza style of cooking can be used for mutton, lamb, goat, beef, fish and vegetable dishes.

● FOR THE RICE

4 rice measuring cups basmati rice

● FOR THE CURRY

800g diced chicken
8 tbsp vegetable oil
1 large white onion, thinly sliced
1 stick 7.5cm/3 inch piece of fresh root ginger, peeled and grated
4 cloves garlic, minced
1 tsp dried fenugreek leaves (kasthoori methi)
2 tbsp garam masala
1¼ tsp ground chilli powder
¼ tsp ground turmeric
1 tbsp ground cumin
1 pierced green chilli
6 peppercorns
3 large white onions, cut in half and thinly sliced
2 tsp tomato purée (heaped)
4 sticks fresh coriander/cilantro, leaves and stalks chopped
1 tsp sugar
200ml water
2 tsp salt

HOW TO MAKE

1. Add the rice (4 cups) to the white rice level 4 line on your rice cooker bowl. Select the 'WHITE RICE' or similar function on your rice cooker. Press 'START'.

2. Add 2 tbsps of the oil in a large heavy pan and put on medium-high heat. Add the diced onion, ginger, fenugreek and garlic and fry for 6-8 minutes or until the onion softens/turns golden brown.

3. Add the diced chicken until it's sealed then add the ground turmeric, chilli powder, garam masala, ground cumin and peppercorns then stir to coat the chicken with the spices.

4. Add the tomato puree, sugar then the water, salt, pierced chilli and raise heat to boil.

5. Reduce heat to low and simmer gently, partial cover for 30 minutes or until the chicken is cooked through.

6. Whilst the curry cooks add 6 tbsp of oil and add the finely sliced onions to another pan.

7. Add a pinch of salt and cook on a medium heat until the onions are completely brown, sweet and tangled.

8. Then when ready stir through the fresh coriander and caramelised onions to the curry and serve with rice.

HANDY TIP! Its important to make sure spices are cooked for at least 5 minutes, otherwise they won't share much flavour to the dish. The curry can be kept in a sealed container for up to 3 days in the fridge or 3 months in a freezer.

PIRI PIRI CHICKEN WITH RICE

The history of Piri Piri is as colourful as the dish itself

Portuguese in origin, Piri Piri can be used as a marinade or sauce. Send your taste buds tingling with our recipe!

2/3   **45"**   **EASY**   **RICE COOKER + PAN**

INGREDIENTS

- **2** chicken breasts sliced into goujon pieces (or 2 halves of a chicken)
- **2** red onions and **1** carrot thinly sliced
- **mixed** fresh peppers (red yellow, orange, which ever you prefer) thinly sliced
- **handful** green beans/french beans and broccoli finely sliced
- **4 large** sliced tomatoes (for serving)
- **2 rice measuring cups** short or long grain rice

FOR THE PIRI PIRI MARINADE

5 cloves, garlic crushed
3 red chillies (as hot as you dare!)
1 tsp ginger, grated or a **tsp** of ready minced ginger
50ml vegetable oil
25ml white or red wine vinegar
3 tbsp soy sauce
1 tsp tabasco (or more if you want it hot!)
1 tbsp smoked paprika
1 tbsp sweet paprika
3 tsp dried oregano
1 tsp caster sugar (optional)
2 tbsp lime/lemon juice

HOW TO MAKE

1. Put the piri piri marinade into a bowl. Add chicken and leave to marinade for at least an hour.

2. At this point make coconut ginger rice or plain long grain rice in your rice cooker.

3. Take 2 tbsp of the piri piri infused oil and heat in a pan and cook the onion for 5 minutes.

4. Add the marinaded chicken into the pan.

5. 5 minutes before the chicken is ready, add the sliced veg to the pan and cook until soft.

6. Serve with delicious coconut ginger rice which goes perfectly with the spicy piri piri flavours or plain long grain (or even short grain) rice if you prefer.

HANDY TIP!

Serve with pita bread for a yummy snack as an alternative to a rice pairing.

Add a splash of Scotch whisky for a lift. Surprisingly it works well.

MOROCCAN CHICKEN AND CHICKPEA STEW

Fragrant spice blends produce a filling meal with several levels

2   **50"**   **HARD**   **RICE COOKER + PAN**

A spicy, fragrant dish making use of fiery harissa paste and ras-al-hanout Moroccan spice blend. Usually cooked and served in a tagine (earthenware pot) but stews perfectly in a rice cooker.

• FOR THE SPICE MIX (ras-al-hanout)

You can buy Moroccan spice mix but we make our own for best results

1 tsp ground cumin and **1 tsp** ground ginger
½ tsp ground cinnamon and **½ tsp** ground coriander
½ tsp ground allspice and **½ tsp** cayenne
¼ tsp ground cloves and **½ tsp** paprika
½ tsp dried onion
1 tsp salt and **¾ tsp** black pepper
½ tsp dried garlic and **¼ tsp** oregano
1 handful fresh basil and **¼ tsp** thyme

• INGREDIENTS FOR THE CURRY

2 chicken breast
1 tin of tomatoes
1 tin of drained chickpeas
1¼ tbsp tomato puree
1 tbsp Moroccan spice mix and **1 tsp** harissa paste (if you don't like it as spicy, then add less)
1 chicken or beef stock cube
1 red onion in chunks
1 carrot in small chunks
1 red and **1** yellow pepper
5 green beans
1 tsp minced ginger and **1 tsp** minced garlic
2 pinches salt, black pepper, **pinch** of sugar
2 tsp lemon juice

HOW TO MAKE

1. Add all ingredients of the spice mix to a jar, mix well. If air tight the jar of mix can be stored for up to two months.

2. Fry the onion and carrot in olive oil, when they are beginning to brown add the garlic and ginger and stir.

3. Add the harissa paste and Moroccan spice to your spice preference.

4. Add a splash of water and then add the chicken. Once the chicken is sealed, add the tin of tomatoes, tomato puree, salt, black pepper, sugar and stock cube. Add a splash of water to loosen the mix a bit so the chicken is mostly covered.

5. Transfer to your rice cooker bowl and press the 'SLOW COOK' function on your rice cooker. Set for around 2 hours cooking time. Press 'START'.

6. After an hour, add the chickpeas, green beans, peppers and cook for another 45-60 mins.

7. Towards the end of cooking adjust the seasoning of the stew and add a good squirt of lemon juice.

8. Serve with long grain rice!

HANDY TIP! Serve with long grain rice, cous cous, a nice warm pitta or flatbread straight from the oven! Making the spice mix yourself gives the dish a fresher and more vibrant taste.

BIBIMBAP (Korean rice bowl)

Bibimbap, sometimes romanised as bi bim bap or bi bim bop, is a Korean rice dish

4   80"   HARD   RICE COOKER + PAN

This kaleidoscope of seasoned sautéed vegetables, Korean marinated beef, and the signature fried egg really seals the deal and will satisfy the most fussy of eaters. Add some of the bright red, spicy bibimbap sauce and it completes the well balanced circular spread.

● FOR THE RICE

2 rice measuring cups short or medium grain white rice

● TO PREPARE

1 cup daikon radish, julienned
½ bunch spinach
2 cups bean sprouts
1 cup carrots, julienned
1 tsp sugar
1 tbsp vinegar
1 tsp soy sauce
2 tsp dark sesame oil
1 tsp salt
2 tsp vegetable oil
225g ground or shredded beef

● FOR THE SAUCE

1 clove garlic, minced
2 tsp sugar
2 tsp soy sauce
2 tsp dark sesame oil

● FOR THE TOPPINGS

4 eggs
1 handful crushed Korean dry seaweed
2 tsp sesame seeds
Gochuchang (seasoned red pepper paste) to taste

HOW TO MAKE

1. Measure the rice accurately and place in the inner cooking pan. Rinse rice under water until water clears.

2. Add water by filling up to the water scale marked 2 for white rice. Cook the rice using the 'REGULAR' or 'SHORT GRAIN' setting and press 'START'.

3. While the rice is cooking, prepare the toppings. Mix ¼ tsp. salt, sugar and vinegar into the daikon radish and set aside.

4. Blanch the spinach. Drain and cool with cold water and squeeze out water. Cut into 3 inch long segments, then dress with ¼ tsp. salt, soy sauce and 1 tsp. sesame oil.

5. Blanch the bean sprouts. Drain and dress with ¼ tsp. salt and 1 tsp sesame oil.

6. In a frying pan, heat vegetable oil over medium heat and sauté carrots for one minute and add ¼ tsp salt. Set aside.

7. In a small bowl, combine all ingredients for sauce. Heat frying pan, sauté ground or shredded beef for 3 minutes, add the sauce and continue to cook until all the liquid is absorbed.

8. Fry four eggs sunny side up.

9. When rice completes cooking, place rice in individual serving bowls. Squeeze excess liquid from daikon radish. Arrange all prepared vegetables and beef radially on the rice.

10 Place one sunny side up egg in the center on top of each bowl. Top with crushed seaweed and sesame seeds. Serve with gochuchang on the side.

HANDY TIP!

Mix it all up for a delicious mess or go full veggie by replacing the beef with king oyster mushrooms and spinach.

CHICKEN WITH CASHEW NUTS

Full of protein this one
will keep you full
for hours

2   70"   EASY   RICE COOKER + PAN

Saucy, sticky, crispy, sweet and savoury cashew chicken! Historically a Chinese and Thai dish and when served with rice from your rice cooker, this recipe is better than a takeaway and is authentic like in Asia.

INGREDIENTS

- **2** chicken breasts (or pork, beef, seafood or tofu, whatever you prefer!)

- **mix of vegetables** (we use red peppers, carrots, green beans, baby sweetcorn, mange tout, broccoli and cauliflower)

- **150g** dry cashew nuts per person

- **2 rice measuring cups** white jasmine rice

- **1** yellow/white onion, finely sliced

- **1** spring onion

- **1 clove** garlic crushed using back of knife

- **2** birds eye chillies finely chopped

- **250ml** chicken stock

- **2 tbsp** Thai sweet chilli sauce and a small amount of Sri Racha chilli sauce

- **pinches** sugar to sweeten

HOW TO MAKE

1. Measure the 2 cups of rice into your rice cooker bowl and fill with water to the level 2 long grain level line. Press 'LONG GRAIN' or 'WHITE' and press 'START'.

2. Stir fry garlic, chilli and onions in a pan/wok until the flavours start to release and then add the chicken. Keep oil to a minimum and add spoonfuls of chicken stock to stop any sticking.

3. Once the chicken is sealed add the vegetables and cashew nuts then stir fry until cooked. Keep adding chicken stock in small quantities.

4. Season the sauce with a generous splash of soy sauce, a dash of black pepper and salt to season. Add sugar (to taste) and the Thai sweet chilli sauce.

5. Thicken with cornflour mixed with water and stir through spring onions.

6. Leave to simmer for 10-15 minutes to develop the flavours. Serve with your jasmine rice.

 If you prefer a vegetarian version substitute chicken stock for vegetable stock and replace the chicken pieces with tofu.

2   70"   EASY   RICE COOKER + PAN

FILIPINO PORK ADOBO

Unlike anything else you will eat in Asia this meaty dish will leave you smiling

This Spanish influenced dish is one of the national dishes of the Philippines. Aadobo done correctly is yummy and can be made with chicken or pork.

INGREDIENTS

- **2 rice measuring cups** long grain white rice
- **350g** pork shoulder chunks (or chicken chunks/boned thigh chicken if you prefer)
- **2 medium** size potatoes (parboiled and set aside)
- **3 cloves** garlic (bashed with back of a knife)
- **1** red onion chopped into slices
- **100ml** soy sauce
- **140ml** white vinegar
- **360ml** water
- **½ tsp** finely chopped ginger
- **pinch** paprika and **5** bay leaves
- **pinch** salt, **pinch** black pepper and **1 tsp** brown sugar to taste
- **1 tbsp** cornflour in water to thicken

HOW TO MAKE

1. Use two rice measuring cups of rice then fill to the white/long grain level 2 in your rice cooker bowl with water.

2. Press the 'WHITE' rice function (or 'LONG GRAIN' setting if you have it) of your rice cooker and press 'START'.

3. In a pan saute garlic, onions and ginger until soft. Add the pork chunks and seal.

4. Add the soy sauce, vinegar, water, bay leaves and paprika.

5. At this point add a little salt and pepper and sugar (usually around 1¼ tbsp). Add the potatoes.

6. Leave to simmer for up to an hour. The longer you leave to simmer, the fuller the flavour.

7. Add cornflour and water to thicken and add more salt and pepper, according to how it tastes.

8. Cook for a further 10 mins - serve with rice

 HANDY TIP! As this recipe is traditionally meat heavy we usually also add carrots and some other veg like red pepper, broccoli and cauliflower, but the dish can be served with just pork.

BEEF RENDANG WITH JASMINE RICE

A Malaysian favourite!

4-6   120"   HARD   RICE COOKER + PAN

Slow cooked beef in coconut milk and spices, this dry curry can be paired with sticky rice or jasmine rice.

● INGREDIENTS FOR THE PASTE

15 dry chillies
6 baby shallots
30g ginger
30g galangal (if you can't find any, add 20g more ginger)
3 lemongrass (use the less fibrous section at the base)

● FOR THE BEEF

1kg beef shin or skirt, cut into cubes, roughly 4cm
60g dessicated coconut
1 stick lemongrass, cut into half and bashed
400ml or **1 tin** coconut milk
250ml water
2 makrut (kaffir lime) leaves, torn
5 tbsp oil

● FOR THE SEASONING

1¼ tbsp chicken stock powder
2 tbsp tamarind paste
1 tsp sugar and **¼ tsp** salt

● FOR THE JASMINE RICE

2 to 3 rice measuring cups jasmine rice and a good rice cooker :)

HOW TO MAKE

1. Make the paste by soaking the chillies in boiling water for 15 minutes then remove the seeds.

2. Peel and chop all the paste ingredients into smaller pieces and blend until smooth.

3. Heat oil in a wok or a heavy based pan. Fry the paste for about 5 minutes until the aroma begins to escape.

4. Add the beef and the bashed lemongrass. Mix well and when the beef start to lose its pink colour add in the coconut milk and water.

5. Bring to a boil and lower the heat to simmer with the lid uncovered. Check occasionally to avoid sticking.

6. Toast the desiccated coconut until golden brown in a pan (5–7 minutes). Set aside to cool. After 1.5 hour, add the makrut leaves and the seasoning to the rendang.

7. At this point it's a good time to put your rice into your rice cooker. If using 2 cups of jasmine white rice then fill to the level 2 line on your bowl. Press 'WHITE RICE', 'REGULAR' or 'LONG GRAIN' and press 'START'.

8. Simmer the rendang for another 45 minutes and the oil will separate from the mix.

9. The rendang is now ready for serving with your rice.

HANDY TIP!

If you feel like a change to plain rice then try turmeric rice or sticky rice. The longer you leave this dish the more intense the aromas and flavour!

POT STICKER DUMPLINGS (Jiaozi)

Packed full of flavour with succulunt pork

2-3 | **65"** | **MEDIUM** | **RICE COOKER + PAN**

Popular during the Lunar New Year season, jiaozi are also a fun and delicious appetiser, dinner food or snack to enjoy any time of year. This recipe includes a homemade dumpling dough and ground pork or meat and vegetable filling that uses the 'STEAM' function of your rice cooker.

● MAKING THE DOUGH WRAPPINGS

185g plain flour
110ml boiling water
1 tsp oil

Sieve the flour into a mixing bowl and add the water whilst mixing with a fork/hand. Once all water is added, fold into a ball and knead for 5 minutes on a hard surface until slightly elastic consistency ('play dough' consistency) – you may need more/less water to get it correct. Once consistency is reached, roll out the pastry to roughly 1-2mm thick. Use a 70mm diameter circular cutter to cut out many dumpling wrappers as possible.

● INGREDIENTS FOR THE FILLING

300g pork mince
½ bunch of coriander
3 spring onions
1 thumb print size piece of ginger
1 clove garlic
5 Chinese mushrooms (optional)

● INGREDIENTS FOR THE MARINADE

2 tsp sesame oil
pinches salt to taste
2 tbsp light soy sauce
¼ tsp sugar

HOW TO MAKE

1. Finely chop all filling ingredients and mix with marinade. Place 1 tsp of the filling in the centre of each circle of dough.

2. Fold the bottom centre over the filling to form a semi-circle and pinch the top tight.

3. Pinch the two corners of the semi-circle together leaving two symmetrical 'Mickey Mouse ear' shapes between your centre fold and the corner folds.

4. Now pinch/fold the 'ears' in towards you to make four layered folds. Tidy up to create a 'half-moon' shape and arrange on a plate.

5. Fill the rice cooker inner bowl with warm water to level 2, add the dumplings to the steam basket in a single layer and and press the 'STEAM' function. Set the time to 30 minutes so the pork is cooked.

6. Heat 2 tbsp vegetable oil in a frying pan then add dumplings base down. Turn heat down to medium and fry until base is golden brown.

7. Consider serving with dipping sauce to really enhance the flavours of the jiaozi.

HANDY TIP! Serve with a mixture of equal amounts of soy sauce, vinegar and matchsticks of ginger. Optionally add minced garlic and chilli oil.

TRADITIONAL CHICKEN CONGEE

The ultimate comfort food that
can be enjoyed any time
by anyone

Made with high quality ingredients and a good rice cooker, this congee recipe can give you a high class result with minimal effort.

2/3   45"   EASY   RICE COOKER

INGREDIENTS

- **1 rice measuring cup** long grain rice (we use jasmine)
- **340g** chicken
- **14g** fresh ginger
- **2** spring onions
- **4 stalks** of coriander
- **pinches** sea salt

FOR THE CHICKEN MARINADE

- **10ml** cornflour
- **15ml** oyster sauce
- **30ml** water
- **5ml** chicken stock
- **30ml** vegetable oil

HOW TO MAKE

1. Chop the ginger, coriander and spring onions into thin strips.

2. Cut the chicken into slices and marinate, massaging the chicken for a few minutes.

3. Add the rice to your rice cooker bowl and fill up to the 'PORRIDGE' level line for 1 with water. Use 1 rice measuring cup to 6 rice measuring cups of water if you don't have a porridge level line in your rice cooker bowl.

4. Add the chicken to the top of the rice. Select the 'PORRIDGE' function on your rice cooker. Press 'START'.

5. When the cooker switches to 'KEEP WARM' add the ginger, salt, chicken stock.

6. Stir well and then garnish with any remaining spring onion.

HANDY TIP! Add a sliced hard boiled egg to the top of your congee for some extra flair and a protein boost. If you can't live without spice then sprinkle some chilli flakes, add chilli oil or try adding kimchi!

ONE POT HONG KONG CLAYPOT RICE

Using the claypot function of some rice cookers this one pot meal is a hearty treat which you always want to eat!

2   50"   HARD   RICE COOKER

A traditional dish that has many versions spanning from Dominican Republic to Spain to Korea. Made very easy in rice cookers with a CLAYPOT function. Ideally the rice cooker should also have a solid ceramic bowl for better effect due to the more porous nature of the bowl material which helps balance liquid absorption during cooking.

● INGREDIENTS

2 rice measuring cups long grain white rice
8cm piece cured pork belly (of char sui pork) cut into strips
3 links sweet Chinese sausage
10 dried shiitake mushrooms (soak in hot water for a minimum of 30 mins)
1 baby pak choi sliced in half

● FOR THE SAUCE

1 tbsp regular soy sauce
1 tbsp seasoned soy sauce (zhēng yú chǐ yóu or you can substitute with kecap manis)
½ tbsp dark soy sauce
1 tbsp fish sauce
¼ tsp sugar
¼ tsp white pepper
1 spring onion (chopped in small pieces)

HOW TO MAKE

1. Prepare the sliced cured pork belly, thickly slice the Chinese sausage and drain the shiitake mushrooms in a sieve (reserve the soaking liquid).

2. Remove the stalks of the mushrooms (you can use these for adding to a stock or soup for extra flavour) and slice into thick pieces.

3. Wash rice and then place into inner bowl, add the mushroom soaking liquid and top up with water to the 2 line on the long grain scale.

4. Use the 'CLAYPOT' function of your rice cooker. You could use the CRUST function (if it has one) at a push instead. Normal cooking time is around 1 hour and 15 minutes. Press 'START'.

5. After 30 minutes cooking add the pork belly, Chinese sausage and shiitake mushrooms.

6. When the cooking cycle finishes, add the pak choi on top and close the lid. Leave for 10 minutes on 'KEEP WARM'.

7. Add the sauce mix to the top of the rice and mix into the rice, mixing the pork, sausage and pak choi in with the rice. Break up the crust into the rice.

8. Serve with a garnish of spring onions.

HANDY TIP! Substitute the pork for chicken or tofu. Leave on keep warm longer if you want a drier claypot experience.

SLOW COOK PULLED PORK

Perfect meaty goodness
...now here's the rub

 6   200"   **MEDIUM**   **RICE COOKER**

A firm favourite for group get togethers. Using the rice cookers sealed style of cooking with controlled temperature and moisture containment when the SLOW COOK feature is used it really brings out the best in the pork meat. What you get is fall-off-the-bone tender meat that is packed with flavour. It makes an outstanding pulled pork sandwich but we like to serve ours with rice to not complicate the flavour profile of the meat that has a great kick.

INGREDIENTS FOR THE RUB

- **2kg** minimum of pork shoulder (or similar cut)
- **1 tbsp** ground black pepper
- **1 ¼ tsp** cayenne pepper
- **2 tbsp** chili powder
- **2 tbsp** ground cumin
- **2 tbsp** dark brown sugar
- **1 tbsp** dried oregano
- **4 tbsp** paprika (best if you can mix smoked and sweet types)
- **2 tbsp** table salt
- **1 tbsp** granulated sugar
- **1 tbsp** ground white pepper

INGREDIENTS FOR AFTER THE RUB

1 bottle good quality BBQ sauce
1 tin (400ml) kidney beans
1 stick spring onion

HOW TO MAKE

1. Mix the rub ingredients thoroughly in a bowl first.

2. Massage the rub ingredients into at least 2kg of pork shoulder and leave it for at least 3 hours.

3. Then put the meat into your rice cooker bowl.

4. Close the lid and select the 'SLOW COOK' function on your rice cooker. Set the time for at least 3 hours and press 'START'. Really you can cook for as long as you want, the longer the better.

5. Once cooked remove the meat from the rice cooker bowl. Shred the meat with two forks and add the barbeque sauce. Voila, you have perfect pulled pork!

6. Serve with freshly cooked white long grain rice and for some added flair you can optionally add some cooked kidney beans with a sprinkle of spring onions. This creates an extra dimension of flavour and an excellent source of plant based protein.

HANDY TIP! Apply rub mix generously and get into all the cracks of the meat. Serve as sliders and add home made coleslaw to freshen it up. We also like it on jacket potatoes!

4   **60"**   **EASY**   **RICE COOKER + PAN**

AUTHENTIC BEEF STROGANOFF

From it's origins in mid-19th century Russia, it has become popular around the world. Pair it with rice for a hearty meal!

Beef stroganoff or beef stroganov is a Russian dish of sautéed pieces of beef served in a sauce with smetana (sour cream) and is a delight with rice!

INGREDIENTS

- **600g** beef fillet
- **25g** butter
- **1** onion, thinly sliced
- **250g** button mushrooms, thinly sliced
- **1 tbsp** Dijon mustard
- **400ml** beef stock
- **1 tbsp** vegetable oil
- **2 heaped tbsp** sour cream or crème fraiche
- **1 tbsp** (or more) brandy (optional)
- **squeeze** lemon (optional)
- **finely chopped** parsley, to serve
- **flaked** sea salt and fresh ground black pepper
- **4 rice measuring cups** long grain white rice

HOW TO MAKE

1. Start early with your rice by adding it to your rice cooker bowl and filling to the white rice level line number 4. Press the 'WHITE RICE', 'LONG GRAIN' or 'REGULAR' function of your rice cooker. Press 'START'.

2. Cut the beef into ½–1 cm thick slices, then slice these into strips about 1cm wide. Season with salt and pepper and set aside for a while.

3. Heat the butter in a large frying pan. Add the onion and sauté for 2 minutes, then add the mushrooms and cook until both are soft. Stir the mustard into pan. Coat the onion and mushrooms.

4. Add the rest of the mustard then pour in the stock and leave it to simmer until the liquid has reduced by half. Stir in crème fraiche and put pan aside for a while.

5. In another frying pan, heat the oil and when it's smoking hot, add the strips of beef and stir-fry until brown (about 1 minute)*

6. Reheat the onion and mushroom sauce, then add the beef. Check the seasoning and add more salt and pepper to taste. If you find the sauce too rich, add a squeeze of lemon.

7. Sprinkle with parsley and serve next to your rice

HANDY TIP!

CAREFUL WITH THIS!

If you want to flambé the beef you can do this at step 4. Put the brandy in a ladle and carefully heat it over a flame. When the alcohol starts to burn off (you will see the fumes), tip it very gently towards the flame and it will ignite. Immediately pour this over the beef and give it a quick stir. Stand well back when doing this and be extremely careful.

A SIMPLE RAMEN

Japanese noodle soup that will please everyone

HANDY TIP! Miso paste gives a fabulous umami hit to the soup so it can be brought together really fast on the slow cook setting. Substitute any toppings you prefer. For a different texture, use thick, chewy udon noodles or soba noodles

2 | **60"** | **HARD** | **RICE COOKER + PAN**

Real Japanese ramen takes years to perfect – chefs in Japan train for years but this is a simple version of that delicious comfort food. There are 3 main elements to our ramen – soup, noodles and topping.

INGREDIENTS FOR THE SOUP

2 cloves garlic
½ tsp grated ginger
1 shallot
1 tbsp toasted white sesame seeds, ground
1 tbsp sesame oil (roasted)
113g minced pork, chicken or turkey (you can also use plant based mince)
1 tsp La doubanjiang (spicy chili bean sauce/broad bean paste)
3 tbsp miso
1 tbsp sugar
1 tbsp sake
960ml chicken stock/broth (each ramen bowl requires about **355ml** broth + more for evaporation)
1 tsp sea salt (use half for table salt) - adjust to your broth
¼ tsp white pepper powder

FOR THE RAMEN AND TOPPINGS

2 servings fresh ramen noodles (**300g** fresh noodles or **180g** dry ramen noodles if you are desperate)
medium braised pork belly (chashu) or sliced chicken or tofu
handful bean sprouts
2 ramen egg (**ajitsuke tamago** - soft boiled eggs marinated in a zip bag with 2 tbsp soy sauce, 2 tbsp mirin and 3-6 tbsp water), you can also just use soft boiled eggs
frozen or canned sweetcorn
1 sheet nori (seaweed) - cut into quarters
4 spring onions, finely chopped
julienned Shiraga Negi (Japanese leek), substitute with the white part of spring onions

For additional garnish (optional)
la-yu (Japanese chili oil)
pickled red ginger (beni shoga or kizami beni shoga)
white pepper powder

HOW TO MAKE

1. Mince the garlic, ginger and shallot and stir fry in sesame oil on a medium heat until fragrant.

2. Add the pork and cook until browned and then add the La doubanjiang and miso and combine well with the pork (make sure it doesn't burn).

3. Add the ground sesame seeds, sugar and mix. Then add the chicken stock and sake.

4. Taste the soup and add salt and white pepper if you need to.

5. Transfer to the rice cooker bowl and select either the 'SOUP' or 'SLOW COOK' function. Set cook time to 1 hour and press 'START'.

6. Prepare the toppings you would like to use.

7. Cook the noodles in unsalted water according to the packet (fresh or dry).

8. Once **al dente**, drain the noodles and split between 2 bowls.

9. Add the ramen soup on top of the noodles and then arrange the toppings on top in a decorative manner (see photo above).

2   55"   EASY   RICE COOKER + PAN

LEMON CHICKEN WITH JASMINE RICE

Tangy mixed with savoury, this one will get your mouth watering

A recipe that started this author's love of rice when looking for a simple dish to cook at university. Tarty, zingy and with the right combintion of ingredients is simple but effective.

INGREDIENTS

- **2 rice measuring cups** jasmine rice
- **200g** chicken or turkey breast
- ½ red and yellow pepper (sliced)
- **handful** of green beans, sliced
- **1 tbsp** neutral oil
- **1 clove** garlic (crushed)
- ½ **tsp** crushed ginger
- **2** spring onions
- **1** yellow onion (sliced)

INGREDIENTS FOR THE SAUCE

- **6 tbsp** lemon juice
- **3 tbsp** soy sauce
- **1 tsp** brown sugar
- **pinches** salt and white pepper to taste
- **1 tbsp** cornflour with **2 tbsp** water mixed to thicken sauce

HOW TO MAKE

1. Put the rice into the inner bowl of your rice cooker and fill to the level 2 with water. Press the 'LONG GRAIN' or 'WHITE' function on your rice cooker and press 'START'

2. Heat a pan with the oil, add the ginger and garlic, stirring to make sure it doesn't burn.

3. Add the chicken/turkey and cook for 5-7 minutes and then add the red peppers, green beans and cook for a further 4 minutes.

4. Add the lemon juice, soy sauce and brown sugar, stir to coat the meat and veg, bring the sauce to a bubble.

5. Add the cornflour and water mix to thicken the sauce – do this a little at a time, stirring the sauce well until you get to the consistency you want.

6. Taste to see how balanced the sauce is – it should be the right combination of tarty and sweet with a touch of salty - adjust the seasoning by adding more soy sauce or sugar, a pinch of salt and some white pepper then serve with rice.

HANDY TIP! Add some chopped fresh red chilli for a spice kick. Baby sweetcorn can add some great yellow colour to this lemony dish.

3/4   90"   MEDIUM   RICE COOKER

ACHARI MURGH CHICKEN
Also known as Rajasthani pickled chicken curry

SPICY

A North Indian curry so-called because it contains pickling (achari) spices common to that area. Slow cooking the ingredients packs a punch and gives a wonderful flavour combo when combined with rice.

● INGREDIENTS

3 tbsp vegetable oil

6 cloves garlic, peeled and left whole

¼ tsp black mustard seeds

¼ tsp cumin seeds

¼ tsp fennel seeds

¼ tsp fenugreek seeds

¼ tsp Nigella seeds (onion seeds)

5 dried red chillies

1 large onion, thinly sliced

3cm piece ginger, grated

4 cloves garlic, crushed

2 tbsp tomato puree

200ml water

500g chicken thighs, skinned (serve with or without bone)

1 tsp sugar

2 tbsp lemon juice

2 tbsp lime juice

1 heaped tsp lime pickle

pinch salt

¼ tsp cornflour

200g natural yoghurt (choose a yoghurt which isn't reduced fat or a thick Greek yoghurt to help prevent splitting)

2 rice measuring cups basmati rice

sprinkle coriander leaves for garnish

HOW TO MAKE

1. Set the rice cooker to 'SLOW COOK' function and add a little oil. Add the mustard seeds and allow them to pop. Add cumin seeds, fennel seeds, nigella seeds, and fenugreek seeds. Sauté for 10 seconds.

2. Add the sliced onion and mix well. Add whole red chilies and sauté for 3 to 4 mins covered or until the onions become translucent. Next, add ginger, garlic, turmeric, chillies, salt and mix well.

3. Add the chicken pieces and stir everything together until the chicken is coated with all the spices.

4. Add ½ cup of water and deglaze the pot. Stir in the sugar, lemon and lime juice, lime pickle and salt to taste. Layer the tomato paste on top and do not mix. Close the lid and set to cook for 60 minutes.

5. When finished cooking add a few spoonful of hot liquid from the cooker to the yogurt and stir (this prevents the cold yoghurt from splitting). Use cornflour if needed for thickness.

6. Add the yogurt to the chicken and mix well. Stir in lemon juice and garnish with coriander.

7. Serve with basmati rice (or pilau rice) and naan.

HANDY TIP! Remember to deglaze the pot after sauté to prevent burning ingredients. The idea is to sauté and not burn. Don't add cold yoghurt to the hot curry but instead add a few spoonfuls of the curry to the yoghurt first to prevent splitting.

SRI LANKAN CHICKEN CURRY (Kukul Mas Maluwa)

Uplifting, fragrant and warming

4   120"   HARD   RICE COOKER + PAN

A dark, intensely flavoured curry freshened by chard and lemons and complemented by coconut and potatoes.

● INGREDIENTS FOR THE CURRY POWDER

2 tbsp basmati rice
2 whole kashmiri dried chillies or **¼ tsp** dried red chilli
4 tbsp coriander seeds
3 tbsp cumin seeds
2 tbsp black peppercorns
1 tbsp black mustard seeds
1 tsp whole cloves
1 heaped tsp cardamom seeds (from the pods)
2 heaped tsp fennel seeds
2 unwaxed lemons zest

● FOR THE CURRY

3 tbsp coconut oil or ghee
3 onions, peeled and finely sliced
6 cloves garlic peeled and finely sliced
3-4cm fresh ginger, peeled and grated
500g chicken (thigh, bone in or out)
300g small potatoes
2 whole preserved lemons, roughly chopped
½ tbsp Sri Lankan curry powder (see above)
400ml (1 tin) coconut milk
400ml (1 tin) tomatoes
250g chard
1 whole lemon

● FOR THE RICE AND GARNISH

4 rice measuring cups white basmati rice
100g cashew nuts
½ tsp dried Kashmiri chilli or a pinch of dried chilli
½ tsp ground turmeric
1 tbsp maple syrup
½ tsp salt

HOW TO MAKE

1. Dry roast the rice on a medium heat in a pan until light brown before adding the spices and chillies. Toast for 3 minutes. Stir in the lemon zest and leave to cool. Grind with pestle and mortar (or food processor) to a curry powder.

2. This is a good point to add your rice to your rice cooker bowl. Fill with water to the white level 4 line and the press 'WHITE' or 'LONG GRAIN' then 'START'.

3. Add 2 tbsp of oil and onions to a pan on medium heat. Cook until soft and sticky.

4. Add the garlic and ginger. Cook for another couple of minutes over a high heat, then add the chicken, potatoes, preserved lemons and curry powder. Cook for another four minutes. Stir a lot.

5. Add the coconut milk and the tinned tomatoes. Simmer for 20 minutes with the lid on, stirring every now and again.

6. While the curry is simmering, toast the cashews in a frying pan over a medium heat until golden, toss in the spices and toast for 30 seconds more.

7. Turn off the heat, add the maple syrup and salt. Scoop the nuts on to a plate for serving later.

8. Pull the chard leaves off the stems, tear the leaves into large bite-sized pieces and finely chop the stalks. Once the curry has had 20 minutes, add the chard and the stalks, and cook for a final 10 minutes, until the potatoes are cooked through.

9. Serve the curry with warm bread and rice, and top with crunchy cashews and a good squeeze of lemon.

HANDY TIP!

Serve with rotis or chapatis for variety. Adjust the amount of curry powder to adjust the spice. If you like thick sauce then reduce the liquid amount. Use an airtight jar to store the curry powder.

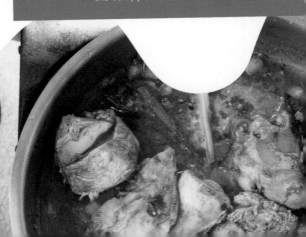

FISH

GOAN FISH CURRY WITH BASMATI RICE

Multi layered flavourful depth.
Hint of tart and sweet from
the onion and coconut

  2

  80"

  MEDIUM

 RICE COOKER + PAN

There are so many types of fish curries in Goa and this is one of the most popular with mutilple layers. It really is delicious and works perfectly with variety of seafood and not just fish – try it with prawns, mussels, clams or squid or if you don't like fish then chicken or/and vegetables can be used.

INGREDIENTS

- **450g** firm white fish fillets, cut into large cubes
- **400ml (1 tin)** coconut milk
- **2 medium** tomatoes, pureed
- ½ **tsp** garam masala + ½ **tsp** turmeric
- **2 tsp** ground coriander + **1 tsp** ground cumin
- **2** mild dried red chillies (more if you like it spicy)
- **7 large cloves** garlic, peeled
- **10g** fresh ginger, peeled
- **2 ½ sticks** cinnamon + **1 tsp** mustard seeds
- **1 small** onion, peeled and chopped
- **2 rice measuring cups** basmati rice

HOW TO MAKE

1. Heat the vegetable oil in a large non-stick saucepan. Add the mustard seeds and once they are popping, turn the heat down.

2. Add the onion and cinnamon. Cook the onion until golden (around 8 minutes).

3. Meanwhile, using a blender, make a fine paste of the ginger, garlic and chillies with 50ml water. Add this to the cooked onions along with the powdered spices.

4. Cook until reduced, then over a low heat cook for 2 minutes or until the oil is released.

5. Add the tomatoes and another 100ml water; cook until completely reduced.

6. Stir in the coconut milk and 150ml water, bring to a gentle simmer and allow the flavours to develop for 20 minutes.

7. Add the fish and cook until done, around 4-5 minutes. Taste and adjust the seasoning.

8. Serve with beautiful long length basmati rice.

HANDY INFO!
Southern Indian curries (like those found in Goa and Kerala) are very different to the northern Indian counterparts. In the South the abundance of coconuts have influenced the food and flavours, resulting in amazingly fragrant but just as tasty curries.

SALMON TERIYAKI

Beautiful fish in this versatile Japanese sauce can be exquisite

2   **65"**   **EASY**   **RICE COOKER + PAN**

Teriyaki is a cooking technique used in Japanese cuisine in which foods are grilled while being basted in a marinade based on soy sauce, mirin and sugar. The flavours are simple but sublime.

INGREDIENTS

- **2 rice measuring cups** short grain rice
- **2** salmon fillets
- **2** spring onions sliced very finely, divided
- **2 cloves** garlic crushed with the back of a knife
- **2-3cm** ginger (around 3-4mm thick), finely sliced
- **5 tbsp** honey
- **1 tbsp** mirin
- **2½ tbsp** lime juice
- **1 ¼ tbsp** soy sauce (start with 1 and add more if necessary)
- **pinches** salt and black pepper
- **½ tsp** of sesame seeds to garnish

*you will need two lots of the above ingredients if you want a sauce with the salmon

HOW TO MAKE

1. To make the marinade combine spring onions, garlic, ginger, honey, lime juice, soy sauce, a pinch of salt and pepper into a bowl and add water. Taste to see if it needs more water, if so add more.

2. Put the salmon into a ziplock bag and add the marinade, seal and leave for at least 30 minutes – the longer it marinades the better the flavour. Make another bowl of marinade for later in the cooking.

3. Stir fry the salmon with a little of the marinade (you can also grill it and baste with the marinade and cook the sauce in a separate pan).

4. Once the salmon is cooked add your second bowl of sauce and thicken with cornflour mixed with water until you get the consistency you prefer.

5. Cook the salmon in the sauce for around 5 minutes and taste the sauce.

6. Adjust the seasoning and garnish with sesame seeds, spring onions and serve with rice.

HANDY TIP! We use honey instead of sugar as we feel this gives a more rounded flavour. We also like to add ginger which gives a little warming kick to the sauce.

COCONUT AND TAMARIND PRAWN CURRY

SPICY

An East African island blend of spice and all things nice

2/3   75"   MEDIUM   RICE COOKER + PAN

Popular in the Seychelles, this curry uses the best spices of the region and showcases them spectacularly.

● INGREDIENTS FOR THE SPICE POWDER

2 tbsp coriander seeds
2 tsp blackpepper corns
2 tsp cumin seeds
½ tsp cloves
6 cardamon pod seeds
1 stick cinammon (or 1 tsp cinammon powder)
1 tsp grated nutmeg
1 tsp chilli powder

● INGREDIENTS FOR THE CURRY

350g king prawns (deveined, peeled and cleaned)
3 tbsp vegetable oil
1 tin (400ml) coconut milk
1 onion (sliced)
2.5cm finger of fresh ginger (peeled and grated)
3 cloves of garlic (finely chopped)
2 green chillies (cut lengthways)
5 curry leaves
½ tsp ground turmeric
3 tbsp tamarind paste
pinches salt and freshly ground black pepper
1 tsp tomato puree/paste (or diced 1 tomato)
2 rice measuring cups long grain rice

HOW TO MAKE

1. Make the spice powder by dry roasting the coriander, cumin, peppercorns, cardamon, cloves and cinammon for 30 minutes until the aroma comes out (don't burn).

2. Grind the spices with a pestle and mortar/processor then add the chilli powder and nutmeg.

3. Add the long grain rice to your rice cooker bowl and fill to the line 2. Use the 'WHITE RICE', 'LONG GRAIN' or 'REGULAR' function and press 'START'.

4. Season the prawns with salt and pepper.

5. Heat the oil on a medium-high heat then fry the onion for a few minutes until soft before adding the garlic, ginger, chillies and curry leaves. Cook until fragrant.

6. Add 2 tbsp of the curry powder before adding the turmeric and tomato puree.

7. Stir gently then pour in the tamarind paste and coconut milk. Allow to simmer for 15 minutes until the sauce reduces.

8. Add the prawns with a pinch of salt and cook for 5 minutes until they are opaque.

9. Season, garnish then serve with rice.

HANDY TIP!

Use a lime cut into wedges and flat leaf parsley to garnish.

Store any remaining spice powder for another meal. It keeps well!

FISH BIRYANI

A spicy fish and rice mix from the Indian subcontinent

4-6   **80"**   **HARD**   **RICE COOKER + PAN**

Aromatic basmati rice blended with fish marinated in warm spices, topped with caramelised onions and coriander makes this fish biryani simply yum!

● INGREDIENTS FOR THE MARINADE

1 tbsp ginger grated
1 tbsp garlic crushed
1 tbsp Kashmiri red chilli powder
1 tbsp ground coriander
1 to 2 tsp garam masala
½ tsp turmeric
1 tbsp dried fenugreek leaves
2 tsp sea salt
10-12 mint leaves roughly chopped
2 tbsp coriander chopped
2 tbsp lemon juice
¼ cup plain yoghurt

● INGREDIENTS FOR THE FISH

900g halibut or mexia cut into 1 inch steaks
1 large onion thinly sliced
¼ cup ghee divided
1 cup chopped fresh dill leaves
1-2 jalapeno sliced into 4 wedges (optional)
1 ½ tsp sea salt
2 cups water
¼ cup coriander chopped for garnish
4 rice measuring cups basmati rice

● INGREDIENTS FOR THE RAITA (optional)

2 cups plain yoghurt
1 red onion finely diced
2 tomatoes diced
½ tsp sea salt
1 tbsp coriander chopped

HOW TO MAKE

1. Make marinade by mixing ginger, garlic, red chilli powder, ground coriander, garam masala, turmeric, fenugreek leaves, salt, mint leaves, coriander, lemon juice and yoghurt.

2. Add fish and coat evenly with the marinade. Put aside in a fridge.

3. Heat 2 tbsp of ghee in a hot pan then add thinly sliced onions and cook stirring frequently for 10 mins or until the onions are caramelised. Take out half of the onion and keep aside for garnishing the biryani.

4. Add 2 tbsp of ghee to the pan with half of the caramelized onions already cooked. Add dill and mix well.

5. Add marinated fish, jalapeño (if using), 1 ½ tsp salt and water. Cook well and season to taste.

6. Cook your basmati rice by adding to rice cooker bowl then filling with water to the white rice level 4. Press 'WHITE RICE' or 'LONG GRAIN' function. Press 'START'.

7. When rice cooking is complete, add the pan contents to the rice and stir well. Garnish with the remaining caramelised onions and coriander.

8. To make the raita, whisk the yogurt in a medium bowl.

9. Add onions, tomatoes, salt and mix well. Garnish with coriander.

HANDY TIP!

Serve with raita (onions and tomatoes mixed in yogurt), lime wedges and even cashew nuts. This is Indian food so use a colour plate to really show off the vibrancy.

ONIGIRAZU SANDWICH

First introduced in 1991 in foodie manga it's an increasingly popular bento choice

2

50"

EASY

RICE COOKER

Onigirazu is made by folding over the nori (seaweed) sheet over the rice, like origami. It's so easy to make this style of onigiri, it's no wonder onigirazu is so popular today. 'Onigiri' takes its name from the Japanese verb for squeezing the rice ball into its iconic triangular shape –'nigiru' – the suffix '-razu' means 'without' doing so.

• FOR THE TUNA/CUCUMBER FILLING

140g tuna in oil, drained and broken into small pieces
2 tbsp mayonaise
1 tsp wasabi paste
pinch black pepper and **pinch** salt
⅛ cup cucumber, julienned

• FOR THE HAM/CHEESE FILLING

2 slices cheddar cheese slices
2 slices ham, thick cut
2 tsp mayonaisse
⅛ cup rocket (arugula) lettuce

• FOR THE RICE

2 rice measuring cups short grain (sushi) white rice
1 tsp white sesame seeds
4 sheets nori (seaweed) 19cm x 20cm size

HANDY TIP! All kinds of fillings can be embedded in rice to create this deliciously compact meal. The possibilities are large with Onigirazu – make it with fried egg and yakisoba/ hamburger and lettuce fillings, salmon and cucumber/avocado and cucumber, minced chicken, cheese and lettuce, tuna and shiso, fried egg and pork, karaage chicken and avocado or simple fried chicken. Garnish with sesame seeds for decorative effect.

HOW TO MAKE

1. Add rice to your cooker bowl and fill with water to the 'SHORT GRAIN' level line. Press 'START.

2. **FOR HAM/CHEESE** - Place one slice of cheese onto the center of the nori. Spread 1 tbsp of rice at the center of the cheese. Place ham over the rice, spread 1 tsp of mayonnaise and top with ¼ cup rocket.

   Place another tablespoon of rice onto the rocket. Using cling film pull two opposite corners of the nori to the centre. Press down to seal the nori to the rice and repeat for the two other corners of the nori.

3. **FOR TUNA/CUCUMBER** - Mix cucumber with salt and set aside for 10 minutes, then squeeze and drain the excess water by hand. Place both bowls in the refrigerator to keep cold. Squeeze out any remaining oil in the tuna with a paper towel.

   (i) Place in a bowl and combine the mayonnaise, wasabi, black pepper.

   (ii) Place a sheet of cling film on a cutting board and place a sheet of nori. Evenly layer 1/8 of rice, half the amount of tuna, half the amount of cucumber and 1/8 of rice. Wrap in the same way as for the ham/cheese.

SWEET AND SOUR FISH

A traditional Thai dish that balances
two of the main tastes of Thailand

2   75"   MEDIUM   RICE COOKER + PAN

Our greedy panda loves the tanginess of this sweet and sour recipe
and how it blends with long grain rice.

INGREDIENTS

- **2 rice measuring cups** jasmine rice

- **400g** good boneless white fish meat (alternatively you can
  use chicken breast, pork, or tofu to suit your mood)

- **¼ tin** or **1 quarter** fresh pineapple (if fresh, use one quarter per
  2 people)

- **1 tsp** cider vinegar, or white vinegar – you can also use lime or
  lemon juice

- **1 dash** Sri Racha chilli sauce

- **2** tomatoes cubed or quartered

- **2 tbsp** tomato ketchup

- **1 ¼** birdseye chilli either fresh or dried (we use two as we like
  ours spicy)

- **1 tsp** brown sugar or honey

- **1 clove** garlic to your own taste

- **1 cube** chicken/vegetable stock diluted with **100ml** of
  hot water

- **1** white/yellow onion

- **1 tbsp** light soy sauce

- **2** spring onions, plus any other veggies you want to
  use (we use, carrots red peppers, green beans, baby
  sweetcorn, mange tout, broccoli and tomatoes)

HOW TO MAKE

1. Add the long grain jasmine rice to your rice cooker
   bowl and fill to the line 2. Use the 'WHITE RICE' or
   'LONG GRAIN' function and press 'START'.

2. Stir fry white/yellow onion with garlic and chilli. When
   the onion is translucent add the fish and cook.

3. Once the fish is sealed, add the vegetables (holding
   back the spring onion and tomato) and stir fry until
   cooked.

4. Add the stock, soy sauce, vinegar, tomato ketchup/Sri
   Racha and brown sugar or honey.

5. Adjust the sauce to your own taste. Thicken with
   cornflour/water mix and add the pineapple, tomato
   and spring onions.

6. Serve with your rice to balance the flavour. Gently
   compact the rice into a small serving bowl and tip
   upside down for a decorative effect.

HANDY TIP! The Hom Mali variety of jasmine rice is
always preferable due to it's purer,
fragrant and delicate texture. When
cooked correctly in a good rice cooker this
rice is absolutely sublime.

2   **70"**   **EASY**   **RICE COOKER + PAN**

BLACK PEPPER SHRIMP

SPICY

Simple but effective recipe that marries with the rice perfectly

Black pepper is a simple seasoner but is very effective as the dish hero (or sidekick) itself. Combine it with seafood to make things really interesting.

INGREDIENTS

- **2 rice measuring cups** long grain white rice

- **340g** shell-on, headless tiger prawn or shrimp, add some black pepper to marinate

- **1 tsp** black peppercorns

- **1 clove** garlic crushed using back of knife

- **1** red onion, finely sliced

- **1 tsp** ginger (small amount sliced finely)

- **2** birds eye chillies finely chopped (if you prefer, reduce this)

- **mixed** vegetables (we use red peppers, carrots, green beans, baby sweetcorn, mange tout, broccoli and cauliflower)

- **1 tbsp** Chinese rice wine

- **1 tsp** honey or palm sugar to sweeten

- **250ml** vegetable stock (if you want to make a sauce of it). Use a combination of cornflour and water to thicken the sauce

HOW TO MAKE

1. Put two rice measuring cups into your rice cooker bowl and fill to the white rice level 2 line with water. Press the 'WHITE' rice function (or 'LONG GRAIN' setting if you have it) and press 'START'.

2. Lightly pound the black peppercorns using a mortar and pestle until they are coarsely cracked.

3. Saute the garlic and black pepper with a little oil on a medium heat in a wok.

4. Stir fry the ginger, chilli, onions and crushed garlic to release the flavour for a few minutes then add the shrimp to cook.

5. When the shrimp is sealed add the rice wine and vegetables then stir fry for around 5 minutes.

6. Add stock, soy sauce, honey, salt and a little more black pepper.

7. Add cornflour mixed with water to thicken the sauce. Serve with white rice.

HANDY TIP! Use a combination of the chillies and black pepper to make it as potent as you like. Have it dry or with a slight sauce. Garnish with a few spring onions and/or lemon to add colour.

KEDGEREE

Popular British recipe originating from colonial India

2   **70"**   **HARD**   **RICE COOKER + PAN**

Tender haddock, golden soft boiled eggs with a touch of spice with a rice base, this is a cherished recipe that has it's origins from the British Raj where it started as khichdi – a dish from the Ayurvedic khichari diet that included spices, fried onions, ginger, and lentils. Those returning from their time in the subcontinent brought the dish to Britain, where it quickly became a national staple, with the lentils usually left out of the preparation and more recently included smoked fish.

INGREDIENTS

- **475g** smoked haddock fillet (undyed and cut in half)
- **2** bay leaves
- **1 rice measuring cup** basmati rice
- **4** free-range eggs
- **100g** frozen peas
- **40g** butter
- **1 tbsp** sunflower oil
- **1 onion,** finely chopped
- **1 tbsp** medium curry powder (heaped)
- **3 tbsp** double cream
- **3 tbsp** chopped fresh flatleaf parsley
- **¼** lemon (use only the juice)
- **pinches** freshly ground black pepper

HANDY TIP! Remember to discard the bay leaves! Use a soft spatula to stir when the fish has been added to prevent breaking the fish. Serve with crusty bread for the hungry eater.

HOW TO MAKE

1. Put haddock skin side up into a frying pan and pour over 500ml water. Add bay leaves and simmer.

2. Cook for 8–10 minutes until it flakes easily. Drain in a colander over a bowl, keeping this to cook the rice.

3. Put the rice into a rice cooker bowl and fill with the drained liquid to the level 1 white rice line.and stir in the rice. Select the 'WHITE RICE', 'REGULAR' or 'LONG GRAIN' function and press 'START'.

4. While the rice is cooking, boil some eggs in a saucepan for around 8 minutes.Cool and peel them carefully and set aside. Cook the peas in a small saucepan of boiling water and drain.

5. Melt the butter with the oil in a frying pan and cook the onion over a low heat for 5 minutes until softened.

6. Add the curry powder and cook for a few minutes. Keep stirring and place the cooked rice into the pan and add the onions, peas, cream, parsley and some pinches of ground black pepper.

7. Flake the fish into large pieces and add along with lemon juice and cook for 2 minutes. Cut the eggs into quarters and place them on top of the rice. Cover with a lid. Heat until the eggs are warm and serve.

MOROCCAN FISH TAGINE

Fish fillets poached in a
spicy tomato sauce, and an
abundance of vegetables
and chickpea.

2-4   40"   EASY   RICE COOKER

This recipes turns your rice cooker into a tagine by using the slow cooking setting. A low calorie Moroccan fish stew flavoured with saffron, almonds, cinnamon, ginger and more. It's ideal for entertaining- make a batch ahead and freeze.

• INGREDIENTS

700g white fish, cut into large chunks
1 tbsp olive oil
1 onion , chopped
good pinch saffron (or tumeric to give the same colour)
600ml hot fish or chicken stock
3cm piece ginger, peeled and grated
¼ green chilli (deseeded if you don't like it too hot), finely sliced
2 tsp ground cumin
2 cloves garlic, crushed
1 tsp cinnamon
1 tsp ground coriander
small bunch coriander, chopped
1 tbsp tomato purée
2 bell peppers (red and yellow)
10 cherry tomatoes, halved
1 zest orange , juice of ½
2 tbsp ground almond
1 tbsp honey
handful flaked almonds, toasted
¼ green chilli (deseeded if you don't like it too hot), to serve
couscous and natural yogurt, to serve (optional)

HANDY TIP!

If you want your tagine to have a bit more kick then consider adding a couple of tablespoons of harissa paste (made from cayenne peppers, olive oil, spices and garlic). You can also add tinned chickpeas if you want more filling. Add at step 4 for best results. Swap the oranges for lemons instead for more zing!

HOW TO MAKE

1. Set your rice cooker to the 'SLOW COOK' function and heat the oil in the inner bowl.

2. Add the onion and cook for a few mins until soft and put the saffron in the hot stock and leave to steep.

3. Add the garlic, ginger and chilli to the bowl and saute for a few minutes more.

4. Tip in the spices and tomato purée, stir for a few minutes until fragrant.

5. Add tomatoes, ground almonds, orange zest and juice, honey. saffron and stock (use all the saffron).

6. Leave on 'SLOW COOK' for 10 minutes (lid open) until the tomatoes have broken down and the sauce has thickened.

7. Add the fish to the bowl, making sure the pieces are all placed under the sauce.

8. Close the lid and slow cook on a few minutes until just cooked (the fish won't take long to cook).

9. Check seasoning, add the coriander and scatter with the toasted almonds.

10. Serve with the chilli, along with some cous cous and a blob of natural yogurt, if you like.

KOREAN KIMBAP CRISPY ROLLS

Different to sushi but of similar origin and equally as yummy

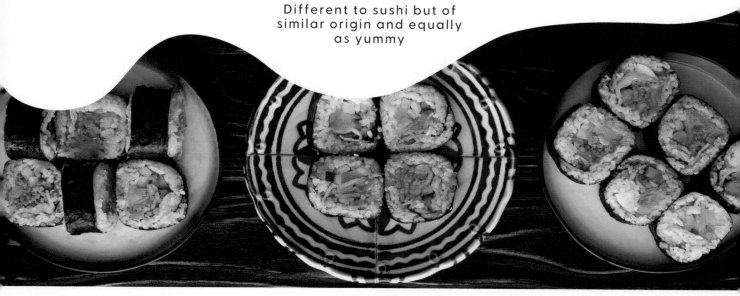

 2

 80"

 HARD

 RICE COOKER + PAN

Gimbap, also romanised as kimbap, is a Korean dish made from cooked rice and ingredients such as vegetables, fish and meats that are rolled in dried sheets of seaweed and served in bite-sized slices

INGREDIENTS

- **6** nori sheets
  2 cucumbers
  1 carrot
  1 pack pickled daikon (Japanese radish)
  2 egg omelette, seasoned with light soy

FOR THE FRIED PRAWNS

- **12** prawns peeled and deveined
  2 eggs, beaten
  300g panko
  200g plain flour
  pinches salt and pepper

FOR THE KIMBAP RICE

- **2 rice measuring cups** short grain rice
  2 tbsp rice vinegar
  2 tbsp sesame oil
  1 tbsp mixed sesame seeds

HANDY TIP!

TO CUT AND PRESENT THE KIMBAP
First wipe off a knife with a wet towel which helps to slice through the roll cleanly. Then, cut down the centre of roll first, then line the two pieces of o ne in front of the other. Cut into three pieces and serve by arranging the rolls to highlight the beautiful fillings in the centre.

HOW TO MAKE

1. Cut the cucumber, daikon and carrots into strips.

2. Put the 2 cups of rice into your rice cooker bowl and fill with water to the 'SHORT GRAIN' level 2 line with water. Use the 'SHORT GRAIN' function. Press 'START'.

3. When the rice is cooked, put in another bowl and season with rice vinegar, sesame oil and sesame seeds.

4. Arrange the beaten egg, flour and the panko in separate bowls ready for coating the prawns. Season the flour with a little salt and pepper and mix together well.

5. To panko the prawns, coat them with the flour making sure to get rid of the excess flour. Dip them into the eggs and finally the panko.

6. Half-fill a large pot, wok or deep-fryer with vegetable oil and heat to 170°C (350°F), or until the tip of a wooden chopstick or skewer starts to fizz after a few seconds in the oil.

7. Fry the prawns, they will take 3-4 minutes to cook (depending on the size).

8. Make kimbap rolls as you would a Hosomaki sushi roll (see end of this section for details) but add cucumber, carrots, omelette, daikon and prawns across the centre of the roll. Cut into pieces and beautifully present.

MEDITERRANEAN PRAWN AND RICE SOUP

A simple warm and hearty recipe than can be enjoyed any time of the year

| 2 | 65" | EASY | RICE COOKER + PAN |

Easily cooked in a rice cooker using the 'SOUP' function this recipe is packed full of prawns and rich flavour along with brown rice as a solid foundation for the other ingredients. What's more, it's healthy which is something positive right?

INGREDIENTS

- **1 tbsp** olive oil
- **675g** raw prawns, peeled and deveined (VEG option: portobello mushroom, aubergine)
- **pinches** sea salt and pepper
- **1 tbsp** olive oil
- **1 tbsp** fresh garlic, crushed
- **150g** white onion, diced
- **1 tbsp** dried thyme
- **1 litre** low-sodium chicken stock (or vegetable stock)
- **1 tin (400g)** chopped fire-roasted tomatoes
- **2 rice measuring cups** cooked brown rice (Use the 'BROWN' rice setting of your rice cooker)
- **2** bay leaves
- **175g** diced bell pepper (use a combination of yellow, red, and orange)
- **800g** raw spinach
- **1** lemon juice, for garnish
- **handful** fresh chopped parsley, for garnish

HOW TO MAKE

1. Set pan on high heat. Once hot add a little oil then a pinch of sea salt and pepper to the prawns and cook until the outside edges of the prawns are seared (or slightly burned), about 6 – 8 minutes, then remove from the pan to set aside.

2. Reduce the heat to medium (you can do this step in your rice cooker using the 'SLOW COOK' function if you wish), then add oil, onion, and garlic.

3. Caramelise the onions (careful not to burn the garlic). Scrape the bottom of the pan if there are pieces of prawn or seasoning left there. After 2 minutes, add thyme and continue stirring for 1 minute.

4. Add stock, tomatoes, and the cooked rice to your rice cooker bowl and set for 30 minutes on 'SLOW COOK'. Once warm add a few pinches of sea salt and pepper and the bay leaves.

5. After 20 minutes, add diced bell pepper and spinach then slow cook again for a further 15 minutes.

6. Season to taste with sea salt and pepper, then garnish with lemon and parsley.

HANDY TIP! You could try and use the 'SLOW COOK' function of your rice cooker to sear the prawns but if you have a pan and stove then this is the better way to do this step as it prevents any damage to your rice cooker bowl and gives a better sear.

SINIGANG HIPON (shrimp in sour soup)

Sour, salty, with a hint of sweet and bitter, Sinigang is one of the Philippine's most loved dishes

4 · 65" · MEDIUM · RICE COOKER + PAN

This soup's flavour is sour with fruits abundant in the Philippines like tamarind, guava, green mangoes or bilimbi (kamias). Add in some big, fresh, succulent shrimp swimming in a savory, sweet, and sour broth...the thought of it will instantly set off any mouth watering.

INGREDIENTS

- **4 rice measuring cups** long grain white rice
- **6 cups** water for boiling the shrimp
- **500g** shrimps (with skin and head), seasoned with a little salt
- **3** plum tomatoes, quartered
- **2** onions, chopped
- **1** white radish, sliced
- **2** mild green chilli peppers
- **6** okra
- **5 ¼ cups** freshly squeezed Tamarind juice or to taste
- **2 tbsp** fish sauce or use Salt instead, to taste
- **280g** fresh spinach or 1–2 bunches of Kangkong
- **3** mini guava (bayabas) - optional

HOW TO MAKE

1. Add the rice to the rice cooker bowl. If using 4 cups of rice then fill up to the level 4 white rice line. Select the 'WHITE RICE', 'LONG GRAIN' or 'REGULAR' rice function and press 'START'.

2. Bring the water to a boil in a large pan then add the tomatoes, onions and sliced radishes and cook until the latter are tender-crisp (half-cooked).

3. Add the green chili peppers, okra, bayabas (optional) and tamarind juice and continue to cook for another 3 minutes.

4. Add the shrimp and season with salt or fish sauce, to taste then cook for another 4-5 minutes or until shrimps are cooked and veggies are all tender.

5. Check the seasoning at this point – add more souring agent, fish sauce or water, if necessary, then turn off the heat.

6. Stir in the Kangkong/spinach and then cover and let it wilt and cook for a couple of minutes. The steam from the hot soup should cook it quick.

7. Ladle the sour shrimp soup into bowls and you must serve with white rice for the traditional broth accompaniment

HANDY TIP! Try with other proteins such as pork, beef, or prawns. Try also with sawsawan, a dipping sauce made with fish sauce, calamansi and some chili.

SAYADIEH

A seasoned fish and rice dish originating in Lebanon. The word sayadieh roughly translates to "catch" as in fishermans catch

4 70" MEDIUM RICE COOKER + PAN

Sayadieh is a classic Middle Eastern rice and fish dish that consists of fried white fish, fluffy spiced rice, caramelized onions, and a tahini salad.

● INGREDIENTS FOR THE TAHINI SALAD

1 cup parsley (finely chopped)
½ cup tomatoes Finely diced
¾ cup Tahini
1 large lemon's juice add more for extra tanginess
½ cup water to thin out salad, add to your thickness preference
1 clove garlic (minced or crushed)
Salt to taste

● INGREDIENTS FOR THE RICE

2 rice measuring cups long grain white rice
1 tbsp olive oil
1 tbsp cumin
¼ tsp turmeric
1 cube bouillon
2 yellow onions (thinly sliced)
2 tbsp olive oil
1 tsp cumin
pinches salt and pepper (to taste)

● INGREDIENTS FOR THE FISH

500g cod, cut into fillets (or any white fish like halibut)
1 tbsp cumin
½ tbsp smoked paprika
pinches salt and pepper (to taste)
2 tbsp olive oil (for pan searing)
handful chopped almonds or pine nuts (for toasting)

HOW TO MAKE

1. Mix together the salad ingredients and then set aside.

2. Prepare the onions by adding olive oil to a pan then the onions and seasonings. Stir and cook on medium heat until onions becomes caramelized and crisp. ¾ of the crisp onions go in the rice and the rest as garnish.

3. For the rice add to your rice cooker inner bowl with all the other rice ingredients and mix together. Fill to the white level line 2 with water or stock. Select 'WHITE RICE', 'REGULAR' or 'LONG GRAIN' and press 'START'.

4. For the fish, pat it dry then season on both sides with the seasonings. Then, add the olive oil to a pan. (Use the same one the onions were cooked in).

5. Apply medium high heat to the pan then cook the fish for 4-5 minutes each side. Be very gentle when flipping the fish. The fish should be seared and cooked throughout.

6. To assemble, add the rice to the servings dish then top with the extra caramelized onions. Add the fish on top of that then add some toasted slivered almonds and parsley as garnish.

7. Serve with the refreshing tahini salad.

HANDY TIP! The almonds or pine nuts should be toasted to a golden brown. The onions should be caramelised to a dark brown. To prevent burning the nuts and onions remove from heat when ready to a paper towel.

2   45"   EASY   RICE COOKER

HAWAIIAN POKE BOWL

This native Hawaiian dish is super-healthy and simple to prepare

A simple definition of poke is diced raw fish because poke means to slice or cut, so that's why almost all poke bowl recipes you see call for diced fish. Much of the time poke is served simply as a starter with just the fish itself, but poke bowl has now been turned into an entire meal with the addition of rice and vegetables.

INGREDIENTS

- ¼ **cup** light soy sauce
- **2 tsp** rice vinegar
- **2 tsp** sesame oil
- **1 tsp** freshly grated ginger
- **pinch** chilli powder
- **2** spring onions, thinly sliced, plus more for garnish
- **1 tsp** toasted sesame seeds, plus more for garnish
- **500g** sushi-grade ahi tuna or good quality salmon, cut into bite-size pieces
- **handful** (optional) ogo (Hawaiian seaweed)

SERVE TO YOUR APPETITE

- **2 rice measuring cups** cooked white or brown rice
- sliced avocado
- sliced cucumber
- edamame beans
- shredded carrots
- sliced radish

HOW TO MAKE

1. In a large bowl, whisk together soy sauce, rice vinegar, sesame oil, ginger, chilli powder, green onions, and sesame seeds.

2. Add tuna and toss to coat. Refrigerate for at least 15 minutes or up to 1 hour.

3. To serve, add rice to the bottom of four bowls. Top with tuna and toppings of your choice. Garnish with spring onions and sesame seeds before serving.

4. Arrange in a decorative fashion around the bowl (see photo opposite).

HANDY TIP! Substitute tuna with chicken or tofu. Serve with wasabi mayonnaise drizzled over for an extra kick (½ tbsp wasabi powder, 1 tsp water, 3 tbsp mayonnaise)

THAI RED CURRY

A spicy, vibrant Thai favourite
which packs a punch of flavour

SPICY

3-4 | **80"** | **HARD** | **RICE COOKER + PAN**

Forget ordering takeaway and make your own Thai red curry at home.
Full of flavour, although this recipe is for seafood you can equally
substitute for chicken, tofu, fish or duck.

● INGREDIENTS FOR THE CURRY PASTE

5 fresh red chillies
5 dried red chillies, soaked in hot water and drained when soft
4 Thai shallots, finely chopped
1cm piece of fresh turmeric
2 cloves garlic, finely chopped
30g chopped galangal, finely chopped
2 stalks lemongrass, finely chopped
30g ginger, finely chopped
1 tsp shrimp paste
4 makrut (kaffir lime) leaves, finely chopped
1 coriander root, chopped
1 tsp cumin
1 tsp coriander seeds
1 tbsp paprika, for a deep red colour

● INGREDIENTS FOR THE CURRY

1 large sweet potato, washed, peeled and diced into large chunks (1 inch)
300g king prawns, peeled and deveined
100g baby corn, cut into bite size pieces
100g mange tout
100g pea aubergines
1 tin (400ml) coconut milk
4 makrut (kaffir lime) leaf (tear off stem)
50g coriander, leaves picked/rough chopped
10 leaves Thai basil, torn
1 red chilli, sliced
4 tbsp fish sauce
2 tsp sugar
oil for frying
3 rice measuring cups jasmine rice

HOW TO MAKE

1. **FOR THE PASTE** - Crush the cumin and coriander seeds
   using a pestle & mortar until finely ground. Add garlic,
   fresh and dried red chillies into the mortar and pound
   well.

   Add lemongrass, galangal, coriander root, makrut
   peel, and pound well. Add shallot, ginger and pound
   well. Add shrimp paste and pound until smooth. Add
   the paprika.

2. Add the rice to your rice cooker bowl and fill with
   water to the white level line 3. Press 'WHITE RICE',
   'LONG GRAIN' or 'REGULAR' rice function and press
   'START'.

3. **FOR COOKING** - Put the oil into a saucepan over low
   heat and add the red curry paste made above. Stir
   continuously until fragrant.

4. Add sweet potato, pour the top third of a tin of
   coconut milk and stir constantly until simmering point
   is reached.

5. Add the remaining coconut milk and bring to the boil.

6. Add the makrut leaves, aubergines, sugar snaps and
   baby corn stirring occasionally.

7. Add the prawns and cook until they change from
   opaque to pink, usually 2-3 minutes.

8. Season to taste with fish sauce and sugar.

9. Add the Thai basil.

10. Pour into a bowl and decorate with red chillies and
    serve with perfect rice from your rice cooker.

HANDY TIP! Add some pineapple chunks from a tin or
fresh. Yes it works! It adds an element of
sweetness that blends very nicely with the
spiciness of the curry.

THAI PINEAPPLE FRIED RICE

A summery and fruit fried rice
- a spin on the usual
fried rice fare

Savoury jasmine rice combined with juicy sweet pineapple and spices sounds like an unusual combination but it makes a terrific tropical dish.

2   45"   EASY   RICE COOKER + PAN

INGREDIENTS

- **1** pineapple
- **2 rice measuring cups** cooked and cooled jasmine rice
- ½ green pepper, diced
- ½ red pepper, diced
- ½ onion, diced
- **2 cloves** garlic, minced
- ¼ **cup** cashews
- **4-6** prawns, raw or cooked
- **1** egg
- **4-6 tbsp** vegetable oil
- **2 tsp** curry powder
- ½ **tsp** ground turmeric
- **2 tbsp** fish sauce
- **1 tbsp** light soy sauce
- **2 tsp** sesame oil
- **pinch** white pepper
- **1** spring onion, finely sliced to garnish
- **1** red chilli, finely sliced to garnish

HOW TO MAKE

1. Slice the pineapple lengthwise to create a pineapple bowl. Cut the interior to make a rectangle and criss cross it to help scoop out the flesh with a spoon. Finely dice the pineapple pieces, and set aside. Chop the rest of the vegetables and set aside.

2. Heat 2 tbsp vegetable oil in a wok on high heat. Add the prawns, cook for 2-3 minutes until they turn pink. Remove from the wok and set aside. Heat another 2 tbsp of oil in a wok on high heat and crack the egg into it, fry until the egg is half cooked, break the yolk and cut into the white with your spatula.

3. Push the egg to one side of the wok to allow space for your rice, add 1 tbsp vegetable oil to the wok and once smoking hot, add the rice to the wok and mix well, trying to separate rice so as to remove any clumps.

4. Once the rice is mixed, add the veg and stir fry until well mixed. Add the curry powder, turmeric, pineapple, cashews and mix into the rice.

5. Return the prawns to the pan, continuing to stir-fry. Add a splash of light soy sauce and fish sauce then season with white pepper and add a dash of sesame oil, taste and adjust.

HANDY TIP!

Decorate with spring onion and chilli scattered on top.

Canned pineapple will also be okay in a pinch. You won't get the same wow effect but it will taste just as good.

BRAZILIAN FISH STEW
(Moqueca Baiana)

Not too rich, this refreshing
dish will transport you
to South America

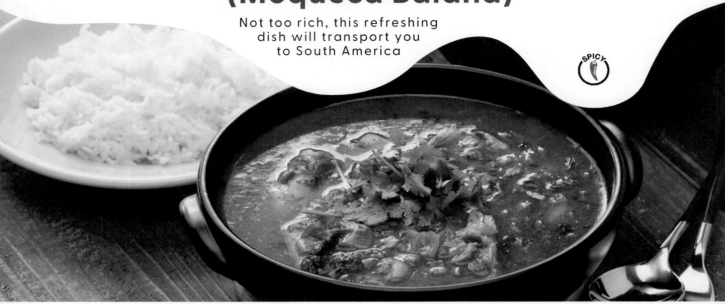

 4

 60"

 MEDIUM

 RICE COOKER + PAN

This traditional Brazilian dish uses a delicately flavoured coconut base broth with a good depth of flavour considering it's relatively short ingredient list! The broth is quite refreshing and not too rich, unlike many strong flavoured, rich coconut based curries. It also works with other seafood.

INGREDIENTS FOR THE FISH

500g firm white fish fillet, no skin, cut to 2.5 cm cubes
1 tbsp lime juice
¼ tsp salt
pinch black pepper
1 tbsp olive oil

INGREDIENTS FOR THE BROTH

1½ tbsp olive oil or coconut oil
2 cloves garlic, minced
1 small onion, finely diced (brown, yellow or white)
1 red bell pepper (large), halved and sliced
1½ tsp sugar (any)
1 tbsp cumin powder
1 tbsp paprika
1 tsp cayenne pepper (optional)
½ tsp salt
400ml coconut milk (1 tin)
400ml canned crushed tomatoes
1 cup fish broth/stock

FOR THE RICE AND GARNISH

4 rice measuring cups long grain white rice
1-2 tbsp lime juice , plus more for serving
3 tbsp roughly chopped fresh coriander

HANDY TIP! This recipe is best made with firm white fish fillets because they hold their shape better. Halibut, cod, hake, tilapia, bass, catfish, John Dory, barramundi or any kind of snapper!

HOW TO MAKE

1. Combine the fish, lime juice, oil, salt and pepper in a bowl. Cover with cling film and refrigerate for 20 minutes.

2. Bring the 1 tbsp olive oil in a large pan to a high heat. Add the fish and cook until just cooked through and golden brown. Set aside.

3. Add rice to your cooker bowl and fill with water to the white level line 4. Press the 'WHITE', 'REGULAR' or LONG GRAIN' rice function. Press 'START'

4. Use a medium high heat with 1½ tbsp olive oil in the same pan. Add the garlic and onion and cook for 1½ minutes or until the onion becomes translucent. Add the bell pepper and cook for 2 minutes.

5. Add the remaining broth ingredients. Bring to a simmer, then turn down to medium. Cook for 30 to 40 minutes or until it thickens. Adjust salt and pepper to taste.

6. Return the fish to the broth to reheat for about 2 minutes. Stir in lime juice.

7. Garnish with coriander and serve with rice.

SUSHI VARIETY
Styles and ingredients

The word sushi may bring you images of fish over a bed of oval shaped rice or a piece of roll revealing rice, fillings and nori sheet (seaweed) outside. While these two are definitely the most popular sushi options available, it's just the tip of the iceberg. There are so many other types of sushi you can discover and enjoy. Here are some of the most popular, but certainly not the full range of, sushi styles that are too numerous to list here.

NIGIRI

The original and most traditional style of sushi rolls that have existed for centuries. Comprising of an oval bed of seasoned rice topped with raw fish, seafood, or vegetables. When you order nigiri, you will be served two pieces on a plate.

MAKI ROLL

Traditional Japanese rolls prepared by rolling a layer of rice with different varieties of fish or vegetables inside. It has nori or seaweed on the outside. The roll is formed in the shape of a circular tube and then cut into bite-size pieces.

URAMAKI ROLL

Also known as the inside-out roll, these are Americanised sushi rolls that are rolled in a different way with nori sheet hidden inside and rice on the top. They are usually decorated with toppings over the rice to make it an appetising treat.

TEMAKI ROLL

Also known as the hand rolls, these are cone-shaped sushi with nori sheet folded like a cone. They contain seasoned sushi rice and a variety of fillings. Can easily be eaten with your hands instead of using chopsticks

HOSOMAKI

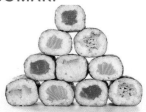

Thin rolls (2.5cm in diameter), with nori on the outside of the sushi rice. Normally contains 1 single ingredient to be the highlight so you can enjoy the fresh, clean taste of the sushi. They should be consumed in a single bite.

POPULAR SUSHI INGREDIENTS

Maguro (tuna) – it implies different species and cuts of the tuna. The common tuna for sashimi/sushi includes **Honmaguro** (bluefin tuna), **Minamimaguro** (southern bluefin tuna), **Kihadamaguro** (yellowfin tuna), **Mebachimaguro** (big-eyed tuna), and **Binchoumanguro** (albacore tuna).
Toro – the fattiest part of a fish, often from bluefin tuna; it is usually the most expensive and sought-after piece.
Katsuo (skipjack tuna) – the most widely available and sustainable type of tuna.
Hamachi (yellowtail fish)
Saba (mackerel) – usually sliced with some skin on one side and served as sashimi.
Shake (salmon) – pronounced as 'sha-keh'.
Unagi (freshwater eel) – unagi is usually grilled and drizzled with a sweet sauce rather than eaten raw.
Tako (octopus)
Ika (squid)
Ebi (shrimp)
Kani (crab) – real crab, not surimi which is made from fish meat to imitate crab.
Hotate (scallop)
Uni (sea urchin)
Tamago (sweet egg omelet)
Tobiko (flying fish roe) – these tiny, bright orange roe are often used as the main topping for sushi, or as a garnish to enhance sushi rolls, or as an outer coating for sushi.
Ikura (salmon roe) – another favorite topping for sushi rolls, chirashi sushi, and sushi cake.

HANDY **INFO!**

You can make Hosomaki with many ingredients. Here are some to try:

Tekka maki – tuna rolls
Kappa maki – cucumber rolls
Natto Maki – fermented soybeans rolls
Kanpyo Maki – dried gourd rolls
Oshinko Maki – pickled daikon roll
Umekyu – pickled plum & cucumber roll
Negihama Maki – yellowtail rolls

POPULAR SUSHI ACCOMPANIMENTS

Soy Sauce – you can use sashimi soy sauce or regular Japanese soy sauce.
Wasabi (Japanese horseradish) – real Japanese wasabi is expensive and hard to find. Very often, the green paste that is served at your local sushi chains or restaurants is not real wasabi. You can buy real wasabi from online shops
Gari (pickled ginger) – also called the sushi ginger, gari is often served and eaten while you eat sushi and it's an essential part of a sushi meal. The lightly sweet, spicy, and refreshing tang of the ginger helps cleanse the palate between pieces of sushi, allowing you to enjoy different kinds of fish and rolls. You can find store-bought pickled ginger or make it yourself.
Edamame – these lightly boiled or steamed soybeans are served as a snack before your sushi is served.
Agari (green tea) – green tea is the most common drink to go with sushi.
Sake – pronounced as 'sah-keh', not 'sah-key', sake is fermented rice wine served either warm or cold.

JAPANESE SUSHI RICE

Colourful, exciting, quirky
and always yummy

  3

  65"

  EASY

  RICE COOKER

The very word 'sushi' means 'vinegared rice'. There are two important factors to making successful sushi rice. First, use a good quality white, short or medium grain rice which will give a soft, sticky consistency. Second, you must use a good electric rice cooker to achieve perfect rice.

INGREDIENTS FOR THE RICE

- **3 rice measuring cups** good quality short or medium grain white rice

- **4 tbsp** rice vinegar

- **3 tsp** sugar

- **1 tsp** salt

TO FILL AND ROLL

Use a bamboo mat and place a sheet of nori seaweed on top. Julienne your vegetables such as cucumber, avocado, asparagus, jalapeño, green onion or carrots.

Have it vegetarian or prepare your fish (thin strips of salmon works well). Spread a thin layer of rice on the seaweed sheet. Place your ingredients and roll the mat, squeeze and repeat. Slice the roll into 2.5 cm thick pieces and serve. We have more about how to prepare, fill, roll and serve in this section.

HANDY TIP! Make it interesting and use low-sodium soy sauce, toasted sesame seeds and/or chia seeds. Lay on some sriracha chili sauce, wasabi + pickled ginger (optional but yummy!). Do inside out roll uramaku with rice/filling on the outside or rolls wrapped with nori on the outside and rice/filling on the inside (maki)

HOW TO MAKE THE RICE

1. Measure rice accurately, rinse the rice under water until the water runs clear and place in inner bowl of your rice cooker.

2. Add water by filling up to the water scale marked '3' for 'SUSHI' or 'SHORRT GRAIN' (note that sushi is short grain rice). Cook the rice using the 'SHORT GRAIN' function of your rice cooker.

3. While the rice cooks, stir the rice vinegar, sugar and salt in a small bowl until the sugar dissolves. Set aside.

4. When the rice finishes cooking, place it into a large, wide, shallow dish (avoid using metal since vinegar may react with it).

5. Pour the vinegar mixture evenly over the rice and mix using a spatula.
   *The vinegar seasoning must be mixed while the rice is hot.

6. As you are folding in the vinegar mixture, fan the rice briskly with a hand or electric fan.

7. Continue fanning and mixing until the rice has cooled to body temperature.

ASSEMBLING SUSHI
Putting the pieces together

There are some basic techniques to follow to assemble your sushi correctly. For this you will need:

· good quality nori seaweed (the best you can buy)
· short grain rice cooked in a good rice cooker
· bamboo sushi mat (makisu)
· cling film
· your ingredients and toppings

HOSOMAKI ROLL (skinny roll)

1. Set up your mat

Place a sheet of cling film onto your makisu to prevent sticking then place a sheet of nori on top of this. If the nori has a shiny side place it face down.

2. Place Nori/rice

With damp hands/wet spoon spread some of your cooked short grain rice leaving a small space of nori empty at the top. Make 3 grooves in the centre of the rice for the fillings.

3. Add fillings

Place desired fillings into the grooves. The fillings can be varied (listed earlier). Ingredients can be cut into small pieces to fit the roll. For Hosomaki it's usually just one ingredient as the focus.

4. Roll and serve

Tuck your thumbs under the makisu, hold the ingredients with your fingers, and roll onto the damp seaweed. Give the roll a good squeeze then cut into pieces (usually 6 pieces for Hosomaki).

URAMAKI ROLL (inside out roll)

1. Set up your mat

Place a sheet of cling film onto your makisu to prevent sticking then place a sheet of nori on top of this. If the nori has a shiny side place it face down.

2. Place nori/rice

With damp hands or wet spoon spread some of the cooked short grain rice and spread it edge to edge. Optionally sprinkle sesame seeds for decoration and flip over.

3. Add fillings

You can now place the ingredients along the centre line of the nori. Tuck your thumbs underneath the makisu and place your fingers on the opposite side of the ingredients.

4. Roll and serve

Roll your mat and nori towards your fingers and apply pressure. Grip the masiku and continue to pull it away from you. Usually for one nori sheet you cut into 8 pieces.

ETIQUETTE OF HOW TO EAT SUSHI

There is a certain etiquette that you should follow when you eat sushi in Japan or dine at high-end restaurants everywhere in the world. Here's a quick rundown:

· First, clean your hands with the wet towel placed next to you before you eat.
· Believe it or not, the proper way to eat maki and nigiri sushi is with the fingers, and the chopsticks are for sashimi. This is not a strict rule so choose what you are comfortable with.
· Go easy with the soy sauce, and pour only a little into the bowl (you can add more later). You're supposed to savour the fresh taste of the fish and rice, not overpowering the sushi with the soy sauce. Look at your nigiri sushi carefully before you dip it in the soy sauce. Some nigiri sushi may have sauce already brushed on top (typically when you order omakase style sushi).
· Dip only the fish part of the sushi into the soy sauce. This flavours it more directly. Avoid dipping the rice as it will cause the sushi to fall apart.
· Do not mix your wasabi and soy sauce together. In many traditional sushi restaurants, the wasabi is already added inside the sushi. Mixing wasabi with soy sauce will ruin both of these flavours.
· Try your best to eat the whole thing in one bite.

HANDY **INFO!**

Uramaki can be pretty when layered correctly. Popular decoration includes tobiko (flying fish eggs (bright red/orange caviar), chives or black or white sesame seeds.

Try making futomaki which is basically a thick version of hosomaki with more chunky ingredients in the centre.

DESSERT

THAI MANGO STICKY RICE

A traditional Thai dessert that is arguably one of the best in South East Asia

4   **55"**   **EASY**   **RICE COOKER + PAN**

Mango sticky rice or khao neow mamuan is possibly THE most famous Thai dessert and it's so delicious, we just had to share it's creation.

INGREDIENTS FOR THE RICE

- **2 rice measuring cups** sticky/glutinous rice
- **350ml** coconut milk
- **6 tbsp** coconut/palm sugar or brown sugar
- **¼ tsp** salt

FOR THE TOPPINGS

- **2** ripe peeled yellow mangoes
- **125ml** coconut cream (you can use coconut milk but will need to thicken this with some cornflour or similar thickener)
- **1 tbsp** palm or coconut sugar (brown sugar will also work)
- **¼ tsp** salt

HOW TO MAKE

1. Cook the sticky/glutinous rice using the 'SHORT GRAIN' setting in your rice cooker. Pour the 2 cups of rice into your inner bowl and fill to the level 2 line with water.

   Follow instructions in your rice cooker manual for sticky rice and which level line to use.

2. While the rice is cooking, mix together the coconut milk, sugar and salt in a saucepan over medium heat.

3. Bring to the boil; remove from heat and set aside.

4. When the rice is cooked, remove to a large bowl and stir the coconut milk mixture into the rice and cover.

5. Allow to cool (or you can eat warm if you prefer).

6. Make the topping sauce by mixing together 125ml coconut milk, 1 tbsp sugar, ¼ tsp salt (and the cornflour if using) in a pan and bring to the boil.

7. Prepare the mango as shown in the photo below and plate the rice, mango and put the pouring sauce into a little bowl.

HANDY TIP!

Make it as sweet as you want by adjusting the amount of sugar.

Top with roasted sesame seeds if you want to jazz things up a bit.

2/3   70"   EASY   RICE COOKER

YUMMY RICE PUDDING

Possibly the best rice dessert ever...

Rice pudding doesn't have to be just for winter. It can be paired with summer fruits in addition to winter fruits for a creamy, light dessert. As easy as, but more tasty than, the tinned version when you cook it in a rice cooker.

INGREDIENTS

- **2 rice measuring cups** arborio rice or other short grain rice
- ½ **rice measuring cup** evaporated milk
- ½ **rice measuring cup** coconut milk
- **1 rice measuring cup** sweetened condensed milk
- ½ **rice measuring cup** regular milk or plant milk (optional)
- **1 stick** cinnamon or ½ **tsp** of cinnamon powder
- **1 piece** lemon zest, one large piece of lemon peel (or orange)
- ½ **tsp** nutmeg and **1 pinch** salt

HOW TO MAKE

1. Rinse the rice in cold water and add to your rice cooker inner bowl with the salt. In this recipe we use two rice measuring cups so fill to the 'SHORT GRAIN' level 2 in your bowl with water.

2. Press the 'WHITE' rice function (or 'SHORT GRAIN' setting if you have it) on your rice cooker and press 'START'.

3. Meanwhile, briefly whisk evaporated milk, coconut milk, sweetened condensed milk, cinnamon, lemon zest (a large thin slice of zest, not grated) and nutmeg to combine together.

4. When cooking is completed and 'KEEP WARM' begins stir the rice once and let the rice cool for 15 minutes by turning off the rice cooker.

5. Add the whisked milks into the rice, close lid and set the cooker to the 'KEEP WARM' function.

6. Check about 30 minutes later and see if it is at the consistency you like. If it's too thick, add some milk/plant milk or more coconut milk to loosen.

7. Discard the cinnamon stick (if using) and the lemon zest and garnish with ground cinnamon.

HANDY TIP! Make it vegan by substituting the cow milk based components with plant milk, oat milk, soy milk or coconut milk equivalents. Blind taste test and you can't tell the difference!

TORTA DI RISO
(Italian rice cake)

A confluence of cheesecake texture meets rice pudding?

6   135"   EASY   RICE COOKER

Room temperature or even cold this Basque cheesecake meets rice pudding is a creamy fragrant rice cake that's soft set and scorched on top. Originally from Bologna, prepared for festivities it can be enjoyed all year round. Arborio rice slow cooked with milk/spices gives a springy soft cake.

INGREDIENTS

- **2 rice measuring cups** arborio rice (cooked)
- **1 litre** whole milk
- **5 eggs** (2 whole, the rest separated to get 3 yolks)
- **200ml** double cream
- **2** vanilla pods, split, seeds scraped out and pods
- **2** lemons, skin finely shaved to get 10 strips
- **1 small** orange, skin finely shaved to get 4 strips
- **175g** caster sugar
- **pinch** salt
- butter for greasing
- **2 tsp** tapioca starch

HOW TO MAKE

1. Cook the rice in your rice cooker by putting the rice into the inner bowl and filling with water to the short grain level 2 line. Then select the SHORT GRAIN rice function and press START. Once cooked put the rice aside.

2. Combine the milk, cream, vanilla pods and seeds, lemon skin, orange skin, 110g of the sugar and a third of a teaspoon of salt, and bring to a simmer on medium-high heat, stirring every now and then.

3. Add the warm mixture to the cooked rice in your rice cooker inner bowl, combine well and press keep warm. Leave for 1 hour and then cancel the keep warm.

4. Allow the rice mixture to cool (take the bowl out of the rice cooker to speed the cooling process) and then pick out the vanilla pods and lemon/orange peel strips.

5. Put the two whole eggs, three egg yolks and 50g sugar in a bowl, add the starch, then beat on medium-high speed for three minutes (use a stand mixer or handheld mixer), until moussy and tripled in volume. Fold the egg mix into the rice in the inner bowl until fully incorporated (it will take a few turns to get it fully mixed in), then put the inner bowl. into the rice cooker.

6. Bake on the cake setting for 60 minutes. Check the cake is firm, if not, then set the cake setting again and cook for longer.

7. Once cooked, leave to cool. When the cake is completely cool, tip out onto a baking tray, sprinkle the remaining sugar on top of the cake and put under the grill or use a kitchen blowtorch to caramelise. Leave to cool until it's a room temperature and cut into thick chunks

HANDY TIP! Add almonds, candied citron, amaretti biscuits (either crushed or whole) and a splash of Amaretto to get extravagant. The biscuits can also work well as a topping or a base too.

VEGAN CHOCOLATE BROWNIES

Decadent and chocolatey just what a brownie should be

 8   70"   MEDIUM   RICE COOKER

An outstanding vegan treat which we searched high and low for and it cooks brilliantly on the CAKE function of your rice cooker. Yes! that's right - a rice cooker due to it's steam cooking process in a sealed unit, is ideal for rich, moist cake baking. This recipe uses an **8 cup** rice cooker but you can scale the ingredients accordingly to the rice cooker capacity you have. It's one of our favourites and popular with everyone who has tried it so what are you waiting for?

INGREDIENTS

- **5 tbsp** sunflower oil, plus extra for greasing
- **200g** dairy free dark chocolate (any good quality chocolate with over 70% cocoa)
- **170g** self raising flour
- **4 tsp** cocoa powder
- **180g** golden caster sugar
- **230ml** unsweetened organic soya/plant milk
- **pinch** salt (sea salt is best)

HOW TO MAKE

1. Break 150g of the chocolate and melt either in a heatproof bowl over a pan of water or by a quick blast in the microwave. Leave to cool a little.

2. Grease your rice cooker inner bowl with a little sunflower oil. Sieve flour and cocoa powder into a large bowl.

3. Add the sugar and a pinch of salt. Stir in the oil, plant milk and melted chocolate until mixed. Roughly chop the remaining 50g of chocolate and stir into the mixture

4. Pour into your rice cooker inner bowl. Smooth the top a little with a spoon and pat the bottom with a flat palm to settle the mixture.

5. Put on 'CAKE' setting for 30-40 minutes. At 30 mins check with a toothpick, if it comes out clean it's ready, if not leave longer.

6. The top will still be quite soft, don't worry about this! Leave to cool, tip out onto a plate, divide and serve

HANDY TIP!
Serve with non dairy cream if you are vegan or dairy if you aren't. Add some fruit or nuts to garnish or drizzle a decorative pattern on top with melted chocolate.

NEW YORK STYLE FUDGE CHEESECAKE

A rice cooker is ideal for making this yummy recipe

8   70"   HARD   RICE COOKER

Cheesecake can be combined with everything from chocolate to blueberries. This recipe with fudge is our greedy panda favourite and made in a **5.5 cup** cooker. **You would need to prepare a base separately for the cake.**

INGREDIENTS

- **200g** cream cheese
- **50g** white sugar
- **30g** sugar (for beating with the egg whites)
- **3** egg whites (separate the yolks)
- **30g** plain flour sifted
- **30ml** fresh cream
- **4 tsp** lemon juice
- **20g** butter melted (use some to grease the bowl)
- **few drops** vanilla extract to taste

HANDY TIP! Pour a chocolate fudge sauce over the cake and add some chopped nuts to garnish for effect. Cut into pieces and you can freeze for later serving.

HOW TO MAKE

1. Soften cream cheese at room temperature or put in microwave for 30 seconds.

2. Grease your rice cooker inner bowl with butter. Place the cream cheese in a bowl and mix with wooden spatula until it becomes smooth.

3. Add sugar, blend with wooden spatula. Add yolks one at a time.

4. Blend in sifted plain flour, fresh cream, lemon juice, vanilla extract and melted butter. At this point add a good sprinkling of fudge pieces.

5. In a separate bowl, beat egg whites until foamy. Gradually add sugar until whites begin to hold their shape as a meringue.

6. Gently fold this meringue into the cream cheese mixture – do this very, very slowly (this makes sure the cheesecake stays nice and light).

7. Pour the batter into the inner cooking bowl and hit the bottom with the palm of your hand to release the air bubbles in the batter.

8. Place the bowl into the rice cooker, close and select the 'CAKE' function. Press the 'START' button and set cooking time to 60 minutes for the 5.5 cup model or 80 minutes for the 8 cup model.

9. When baking completes, allow to cool then place hand on top of cheesecake inside pan and carefully tip out, then slip it onto a ready made sweet pastry case or onto a biscuit base.

10. You can either serve as is or pour a chocolate fudge sauce over the cake. This fudge cheesecake can be cut into portions and frozen successfully.

SPICED APPLE CAKE

A wonderfully moist, tasty cake that can be paired perfectly with coffee

🍴🍽️🔪	🕐	👨‍🍳	🍚
8	80"	MEDIUM	RICE COOKER

A lovely, delicately spiced apple cake which just has to be good for you – it has apples in it! Perfect with custard, ice cream or whipped cream, this is a no-fuss dessert which will wow everyone who tries it! If you don't want to make the effort of making the batter yourself, you can buy a standard cake mix and just add the 2 tsp of mixed spice. This recipe is for an **8 cup** rice cooker. You can scale ingredients to suit your rice cooker capacity accordingly.

INGREDIENTS

- **275g** plain flour
- **220g** brown sugar
- **120ml** milk (dairy or plant)
- **2 tbsp** cornflour
- **110g** butter, room temperature plus a little for greasing (or 100ml of oil)
- **1 whole** apple - very thinly sliced
- **2 tsp** baking powder and **¼ tsp** salt
- **1 ¼ tsp** ground ginger and **2 tsp** mixed spice (made from ⅓ tsp cinnamon, ¼ tsp nutmeg, ¼ tsp all spice and ¼ tsp ground cloves)
- **2 eggs** at room temperature
- **1 tsp** vanilla (this is optional)

> Make it vegan by switching to non dairy equivalents and flax egg (e.g.100ml of oil can be used instead of butter)

HOW TO MAKE

1. Combine all dry ingredients into mixing bowl. Be sure to remove any lumps.

2. Cream butter until light and fluffy (you can use a hand mixer or stand mixer for this!). With the mixer on low, start by alternating the dry mixture and the egg mixture. Pour ⅓ of the dry mixture into the creamed butter, then add ½ of the egg mixture. Alternate until all ingredients used. Stir by hand to fully combine.

3. Grease rice cooker inner bowl with butter (make sure this goes halfway up the inner bowl). Arrange thin apple slices on the bottom in a pretty pattern and pour half of the mixture on top.

4. Tap the bottom of the inner bowl with your palm to dislodge bubbles. Add the remaining sliced apples and cake mixture.

5. Pat bowl again thoroughly then put in rice cooker. Select the 'CAKE' function and the time for 45 minutes and press 'START'.

6. Leave to cool then empty onto plate. Invert the cake to serve to really show off the pretty apple effect.

-91-

PINA COLADA UPSIDE DOWN CAKE

A lighter tropical themed cake
for those breezy summer days

8   80"   **HARD**   **RICE COOKER + PAN**

We take a standard upside down pineapple cake, turn up the tropical and add some coconut making this a super dairy free treat! This is made in an **8 cup rice cooker**

• INGREDIENTS FOR PINEAPPLE

1 pineapple, cored and cut into rings, use enough to cover the bottom of your rice cooker bowl
1 stick cinnamon
4 cloves
2 tbsp brown sugar

• WET INGREDIENTS

4 eggs, separate the whites from the yolks
¼ cup sugar
50ml coconut oil
¼ cup coconut milk
1 tsp vanilla essence

• DRY INGREDIENTS

1 cup plain flour, sifted
1 tsp baking powder
¼ tsp salt

• CARAMEL POURING SAUCE

Combine **1 cup** sugar with **60ml** water in a stainless steel pan until the sugar dissolves and liquid thickens.
Once it changes colour...serve

HOW TO MAKE

1. Place the pineapple, cinnamon, cloves and brown sugar in a pan and cook on low heat until the sugar bubbles.

2. Once pineapple is softer but still firm, turn off the heat and set aside to soak up the juice.

3. In a mixing bowl, whisk egg whites until medium peak while adding the sugar slowly.

4. One by one (mixing completely before adding the next) add the egg yolks, coconut oil, coconut milk, and vanilla essence into the egg whites.

5. Carefully fold the dry ingredients with the wet ingredients with a spatula. Do not overdo this part and make sure that everything is well combined.

6. Place the pineapple rings in the bottom of your rice cooker bowl and reserve the cooking liquid to one side.

7. Pour the batter to completely cover the pineapples. Lightly pat the bottom of the bowl.

8. Close the lid and select the 'CAKE' function and set for 50 minutes. Press 'START'

9. Once complete test the cake is done by inserting a toothpick into the cake. If the toothpick comes out clean, it is done.

10. Remove the rice cooker inner bowl, put a plate on top of the bowl and flip upside down carefully. The cake should drop onto the plate.

HANDY TIP! If you like the flavour of coconut then add desiccated coconut to the mix or sprinkle on top at the end or even serve with coconut ice cream

SOFT CINNAMON APPLES

A versatile sweet tarty soft apple dessert that marries tarty and sweet together oh so well

4

75"

EASY

RICE COOKER

This is one of those 'use it as you want it' kind of recipes. The kind where you can put the soft spiced apples as an accompaniment with oats, granola, pancakes or simple ice cream. Apples and cinnamon are a winning combination and with the tarty comes the counterbalance of the sweet honey. To add some warmth we introduce nutmeg and cinnamon to add some woody and dry spiced tones to the sweetness.

INGREDIENTS

- **6** tart apples, such as Granny Smith apples, peeled, cored, and chopped into half moon pieces (pink lady apples also work second best)

- **3 tbsp** honey

- **½ cup** brown sugar

- **1 tbsp** cinnamon

- **¼ tsp** nutmeg

- **3 tbsp** cornstarch

- **2 tbsp** butter

- **2 tbsp** chopped nuts such as walnuts (optional)

HOW TO MAKE

1. Cover the inner bowl with a very fine layer of olive oil

2. Get a large bowl add all the ingredients except for the butter and nuts, and mix until the apples are coated evenly.

3. Add the mixture to your rice cooker inner bowl and close the lid.

4. Select SLOW COOK function and set the timer to 50 minutes. Press START.

5. When the cooking is completed, open the rice cooker and stir in the butter (and nuts if included). Close the lid and leave for 10 minutes.

6. Serve in pancakes, with ice cream or cream, with granola or oats, as part of a crumble or similar.

HANDY TIP! Walnuts add an interesting crunch to the soft mix along with a good protein hit but be careful of serving to anyone with nut allergies.

BLUEBERRY MUFFIN CAKE

A fun bake that is made in a rice cooker and delightful with hot coffee or tea

6   65"   HARD   RICE COOKER

This blueberry muffin cake is quick and easy with a moist and tender center bursting with blueberries. Super easy to make in a rice cooker and vegan too! For this recipe we used an **8 cup capacity rice cooker** but you can scale the ingredients accordingly to your rice cooker size.

INGREDIENTS

- **1 (baking) cup** flour (gently scooped and levelled)
- **1 tsp** baking powder
- **⅓ tsp** fine sea salt
- **½ cup** granulated sugar
- **¼ cup** tasteless oil (like canola)
- **1** egg or egg replacer/flax egg
- **¼ cup** unsweetened soy, oat or almond milk
- **1 cup** frozen or fresh blueberries

HOW TO MAKE

1. In a large bowl, mix together the flour, baking powder, salt, and sugar.

2. To the flour mixture, add the oil, the egg, and the plant milk. Mix together, the mixture will be stiff.

3. Add in the frozen blueberries and gently fold into the muffin batter. It will tint the batter blue/purple.

4. Grease the rice cooker inner bowl with a little oil and add the muffin batter to the bowl.

5. Press the batter down to cover the bottom of the bowl.

6. Close the lid, select the 'CAKE' function.

7. Cook for 40 minutes, check to see if it's cooked with a toothpick (if it comes out clean, it's ready). If it's not cooked, cook for a further 10 minutes.

8. Garnish with fresh blueberries.

HANDY TIP! Fresh or frozen blueberries work in this recipe. It's tricky to find sweet fresh blueberries all year round. Add when frozen for the very best results

BANANA CAKE IN A RICE COOKER

Moist healthy(ish) goodness

 8   80"   MEDIUM   RICE COOKER

When made in a rice cooker the finished cake is moist and full of flavour because all the banana yummyness gets sealed in! This is a great way to use those very ripe bananas you have laying around. The banana element adds some fruity vitamins to your dessert and is obviously amazing.

INGREDIENTS

- **3** eggs
- **110g** white sugar
- **110g** melted butter
- **200g** very ripe bananas (no skin weight)
- **160g** plain flour
- **¾ tsp** baking powder
- **¾ tsp** baking soda
- **¼ tsp** salt
- **butter** for greasing the inner bowl

HOW TO MAKE

1. Sift the flour, baking powder, baking soda and salt in a big bowl, set aside.

2. Melt the butter and sugar in a non-stick pot and set aside to cool. Mash the bananas with a fork and set aside.

3. Add the beaten eggs to melted butter and sugar. Mix well using a whisk/spatula.

4. Add mashed bananas. Mix with spatula and fold in sifted flour mixture.

5. Pour the cake batter into the greased rice cooker bowl. Pat the bottom of the rice cooker bowl to remove any air bubbles.

6. Select the 'CAKE' function and cook for 50 minutes. It may need longer than this, so test the top of the cake by gently pressing it. If it feels firm, it's ready.

7. Allow the cake to cool for a while in the bowl. The bottom of the cake will have a lovely crust. Plate with banana topping.

HANDY TIP! Serve with whipped cream, ice cream, caramel sauce or just eat by itself for a yummy afternoon treat with a cup of tea! If you are feeling really lazy then just use pre-made cake mix but fresher is always better.

CHAMPORADO (Filipino chocolate rice porridge)

A rich, sweet, but not sickly, breakfast meal to get your day started or to use as a dessert

100% VEGAN

2/3   45"   EASY   RICE COOKER

Usually paired with tuyo (dried salted fish) for that breakfast of champions! We aren't keen on the salted fish so just the chocolate porridge for us!

INGREDIENTS

- **1 tin (400ml)** cocount milk
- **1 rice measuring cup** sticky/glutinous rice
- **¼ cup** high quality cocoa powder (NOT drinking chocolate powder which is different)
- **2 tbsp** dark chocolate (70-90% cocoa)
- **3 tbsp** dark brown sugar
- **1 tbsp** light brown or white sugar
- **pinch** salt

HOW TO MAKE

1. Put the sticky/glutinous rice into the inner bowl of your rice cooker and add the appropriate amount of water (follow the guidance in the rice cooker manual)

2. Add the cocoa powder, dark chocolate and dark brown sugar and stir.

3. Cook the rice on the 'SHORT GRAIN' function of your rice cooker and press 'START'

4. When the rice has completed cooking, add the coconut milk – add half first, then add more bit by bit to get the consistency you like. Add salt and stir well.

5. Taste, if it's not sweet enough add the additional light brown or white sugar

HANDY TIP!

Serve with a drizzle of coconut milk or cherries/other fruit on top.

Add some coffee for a bit of a caffeine boost and zing!

STEAMED EGG CUSTARD PUDDING

This popular Cantonese dessert is simple and you can get inventive with it

2/3 **40"** **EASY** **RICE COOKER + PAN**

Make the egg custard base in your rice cooker then let your imagination run crazy for the toppings!

INGREDIENTS FOR EGG CUSTARD

- **75g** caster sugar
- **2 large** free-range eggs, beaten
- **125ml** full-fat milk
- ¼ **tsp** vanilla extract

HOW TO MAKE

1. Put the caster sugar in a small saucepan and add 5 tbsp of water. Warm through gently just until the sugar dissolves, then pour into a measuring jug.

2. Once the sugar syrup has cooled a little, add the eggs, milk and vanilla. Beat lightly with a fork, without introducing too many air bubbles.

3. Strain through a sieve into a jug. Place a piece of kitchen paper on the surface of the custard mixture to lift any stray bubbles, then discard.

4. Pour custard into four 175ml/6fl oz ramekins, filling roughly halfway up then put into your rice cooker inner bowl. Fill the inner bowl with water up to 2/3 of the outside of the ramekins.

5. Cover the ramekins with a piece of foil and then select 'STEAM' function then press 'START'. Steam for about 25 minutes*, or until just set. When ready, the custards should still have a slight wobble.

   *note that the steam countdown clock won't start until the water has reached the correct temperature

IDEAS FOR TOPPINGS

- Try a cherry jam (pitted cherries in a saucepan with lemon juice and 25g of brown sugar).

- Add some crunch with digestive biscuits or your favourite biscuit. Sprinkle some cinammon to elevate the flavour of the custard

- Try adding some ginger spices if you like more of a chest warming custard.

- It can be tricky but a caramel sauce would balance the egg custard perfectly.

- Grated chocolate and icing sugar for the sweeter tooths also works.

- Keep imagining as the custard base allows for almost foolproof experimentation.

HANDY TIP!
Replace milk with coconut or plant based milk for a non dairy alternative.

Use shortbread biscuits as a dipper. It works!

8   60"   EASY   RICE COOKER

JAPANESE PANCAKE

Feel like an indulgent breakfast or dessert?

This enormous pancake is made in a rice cooker! No need to stand over the stove and flip individual pancakes. Instead, just pour in the batter and let the rice cooker do the work. This recipe is for an **8 cup capacity** rice cooker so scale accordingly to your cooker size.

INGREDIENTS

- **2 cups** plain flour
- **2 ¼ tsp** baking powder
- **2 tbsp** granulated white sugar
- **2 large** eggs
- **1 ¼ cups** milk (dairy or plant)
- **butter** (dairy free or normal) for greasing the inner bowl

HOW TO MAKE

1. In a large mixing bowl whisk together eggs and milk until completely blended.

2. Add in remaining ingredients and whisk until only small lumps remain.

3. Grease the interior of the rice cooker inner bowl. Make sure you go up half way.

4. Pour in the batter and make sure it doesn't reach past the half way mark as it will rise when cooking.

5. Pat the bottom of the inner bowl with the flat of your palm to evenly distribute the mixture.

6. Select the 'CAKE' function and set cooking time for 40 minutes. Press 'START'.

7. When cooking is finished it will have slightly pulled away from the edges of the bowl and should be firm to the touch with a slight bounce back. Use a toothpick to test inside. If there is no mixture on the toothpick then it is ready.

8. Let it cool for a few minutes then invert onto a plate.

9. Serve with berries, then top with a sprinkle of icing sugar and/or honey.

HANDY TIP! It's easy to make this recipe dairy free. Just substitute the milk and butter with soy, oat, almond milk or even coconut milk. It's difficult to tell the difference from dairy.

TRADITIONAL YORKSHIRE PARKIN

Sticky ginger cake made for those winter nights and hot drinks

6   75"   HARD   RICE COOKER + PAN

Up north, in the UK this sticky sweet slightly spicy cake is named Parkin. It's not too dissimilar to gingerbread but has a softer stickier texture and the addition of the absolutely essential oats which gives the cake a grainier more wholesome and chewier texture.

INGREDIENTS

- **120g** treacle
- **80g** golden syrup
- **170g** butter (dairy or dairy free), plus extra to grease
- **200g medium** oatmeal (not the same as the rolled oats usually be found in health food shops; if you prefer a rougher texture, use coarse oatmeal instead
- **200g** wholemeal flour
- **3 tsp** ground ginger
- **⅛ tsp** ground nutmeg
- **175g** soft dark brown sugar
- **⅛ tsp** fine salt
- **1 ½ tsp** bicarbonate of soda
- **1 whole** egg
- **45ml** milk (dairy or plant milk)

HOW TO MAKE

1. Weigh out the treacle, syrup and butter into a medium saucepan and place on a medium heat, stirring occasionally, until melted together. Do not let the mix come to a boil.

2. Grease the rice cooker inner bowl.

3. Combine the flour, oatmeal, spices, sugar, salt and bicarb in a large bowl and whisk to mix.

4. Pour the treacle mixture into the dry ingredients, stirring until no more dry pockets of flour are visible.

5. Beat the egg with the milk, then stir into the cake mixture to create a batter that's loose enough to pour into the tin – if it's still a bit too thick, add a little more milk.

6. Pour the mixture into the inner bowl, level the top, then select the 'CAKE' setting and set the cooking time for 60 minutes. Press 'START'.

7. At the end of the cooking cycle, check it's just firm in the centre and the cake springs back when pressed with a finger (carefully!).

8. Cut into squares or rectangle and enjoy!

HANDY TIP!

Parkin is one of those cakes that gets better with age so stick it in a tin and it will keep for at least a couple of weeks.

For the dairy free people it's very easy to swap out the dairy for plant based substitutes.

SUMAN MALAGKIT WITH COCONUT CARAMEL SAUCE

This Filipino sticky snack or dessert can wow because of it's simplicity

4	90"	EASY	RICE COOKER + PAN

Suman Malagkit is a Filipino dessert made from glutinous rice cooked in sweetened coconut milk with a pinch of salt until almost cooked. The mixture is wrapped in banana leaves and then boiled or steamed until soft and chewy. The sticky rice wrapped tight in banana leaves is usually served with brown sugar, latik, caramel sauce, or with juicy mangoes. It's a filling snack or dessert and delicious with a cup of hot chocolate, coffee, or tea.

INGREDIENTS

- **1 tin (400ml)** coconut milk
- **1 cup** sugar
- **1 tsp** salt
- **3 rice measuring cups** glutinous rice
- **sheets** undried green banana leaves

FOR THE CARAMEL SAUCE

- **1 tin (400ml)** coconut milk
- **1 cup** brown sugar
- **½ tsp** salt

HANDY TIP! Add knotted pandan leaf for a more fragrant rice (if you like the smell of pandan that is). Store for 3 days in an airtight container of freeze for up to 3 months. Reheat by steaming for 3-5 minutes or reheat in microwave.

HOW TO MAKE

1. Prepare banana leaves by trimming stiff ends. Cut into 10 x 10 inch squares. If leaves feel stiff, briefly pass over steam for about 10 to 20 seconds until soft.

2. In a pot, combine coconut milk, sugar, and salt. Stir until sugar and salt are dissolved. Add rice and stir, put into the rice cooker bowl. Select 'SHORT GRAIN' function and 'START'.

3. 10 minutes before the end of cooking stop the rice cooker. Allow to cool. Place about 2 to 3 heaped tbsp on a banana leaf and shape into logs, leaving about 1 inch on sides. Roll banana leaves tightly around the rice to form a log and fold end to seal. You can use string to keep it together.

4. Fill rice cooker bowl to the level 2 with water and set to 'STEAM' function. Set for 30-40 minutes and press 'START'. In the steaming basket arrange suman folded side down. Top with a layer of banana leaves.

5. To serve, peel leaves (make sure the rice is soft and chewy) and drizzle suman with coconut caramel sauce.

FOR THE CARAMEL SAUCE

In a saucepan over medium heat, combine coconut milk, brown sugar, and salt and whisk together until sugar and salt are dissolved.
Bring mixture to a boil. Continue to cook, stirring regularly, for about 20 to 25 minutes or until mixture is reduced and thickened.

HOMEMADE YOGHURT

Culture your own in your rice cooker
if it has a yoghurt function

4   360"   MEDIUM   RICE COOKER

Yoghurt making is something that rice cookers can be uniquely good at if yours has this function due to the way that a constant temperature can be maintained in a dark environment. It takes all of the hard work out of producing perfect, creamy, tasty yoghurt and the best thing is, there is no added sugar or additives so you know exactly what you are eating.

INGREDIENTS

- **110g** plain, live yoghurt (if you want to use probiotic yoghurt, this is ok too) - this is your 'starter'

- **400ml** UHT full fat milk (UHT is best as it has already been heated to a high temperature)

- Fruit, nuts, oats for garnishing

HANDY TIP!

ALTERNATIVE STARTERS
Instead of the plain, live yoghurt you can also use specialised starters that you can buy in powdered form from health food shops and online.

Surprisingly, you can also use chilli stalks (i.e. the green part that holds the chilli to the plant which you discard) as a yoghurt starter. Chilli stalks contain bacteria lactobacillus and 10-15 chilli stalks in place of a yoghurt or powdered starter work to develop any kind of milk into yoghurt.

HOW TO MAKE

1. Combine the yoghurt and the milk together and place in the inner bowl of your rice cooker

2. Close the lid and select the 'YOGHURT' function. Normal cook time is around 8 hours but you can reduce the cooking time down to 6 hours or up to 12 hours; the longer the cooking time, the thicker the yoghurt, the shorter the cooking time, the thinner the yoghurt.

3. The rice cooker will beep when finished. Allow the yoghurt to cool and decant into containers to keep in the fridge.

OUR TIPS!

- Use yoghurt pots instead if you prefer, if you do this then fill the inner bowl to half way up the pots with hot water so the water conducts the heat to the pots.

- For non dairy yoghurts, use a milk which has as few additives as possible (e.g. soy milk without sugar or vanilla).

- If your yoghurt is too thin next time you may need to add more 'starter' and also add 2 tbsp of full fat milk powder and mix well with the milk before adding the starter. UHT milk is used because it has already been heated to a high temperature, but sometimes milk powder and more starter may be required.

- Always add flavour after the yoghurt has finished developing. If you are retaining some to use as your next starter, set this aside in a separate pot before you add anything else to the yoghurt.

- You can top with frozen or fresh berries, use plain on granola or muesli for breakfast.

- Add the yoghurt to thick, fruity jam (always add the yoghurt to the jam, it combines better this way) Maybe drizzle with honey and serve with roasted figs or other fresh fruit.

- Add honey for a little more sweetness or some vanilla.

OATMEAL PORRIDGE

Easier to make in a rice cooker. Add the ingredients, set the timer and you are ready

2   **70"**   **EASY**   **RICE COOKER**

What we love about oatmeal is that it's really quick and easy to make, you can customise it with any toppings, and it keeps you full with lots of energy to last your morning! Add it to your daily routine and you will see how good it makes you feel.

INGREDIENTS

- **1 rice measuring cup** steel cut oats* or similar large rolled oats. Shake well in a sieve **(important to do this)**

  *You may need to experiment with the amounts of oats and water, depending on whether you like thick or thin oat porridge!

- **3 rice measuring cups** water

- **1 rice measuring cup** half cream and half milk (or 1 rice measuring cup of milk). Can use dairy or non-dairy milk.

- **3 tbsp** (or less/more to your own taste) honey or brown sugar

- **fresh or dried fruit** such as banana, apple, cranberries, raisins or mango. Nuts and seeds such as almond/ walnuts for protein!

  (quantities provided here are for cooking in a 5-8 cup rice cooker, scale accordingly for other size rice cookers)

HOW TO MAKE

1. Place the sieved oats and water in the rice cooker inner bowl.

   NOTE: Do not use milk to cook the oats, this will result in a 'boil over' of the contents as milk reacts differently when heated. Only use water to cook the oats.

2. Place the inner bowl in the main body of the rice cooker, plug in the unit, select the 'PORRIDGE' function and press the 'START' button.

3. When the rice cooker turns to 'KEEP WARM' open the lid, stir and add the remaining ingredients.

   Using the timer function and soaking the oats overnight will help soften the texture.

4. Add any dried or fresh fruit to the porridge instead of sugar – delicious and healthy on a cold winter's day!

   See the following page for some porridge topping ideas to help you get creative!

HANDY TIP! Add spices such as cinnamon, cardamom, nutmeg, pumpkin spice or ginger to liven it up. Splash a dollop of milk, cream or yoghurt if you like it creamy! If you like it sweeter try honey, maple syrup or agave syrup.

PORRIDGE TOPPINGS

Inventive toppings for your morning bowl of oats, why should breakfast be boring?

Porridge with amazing toppings can banish the winter blues and keep you full up until lunch. Cooking oat porridge in a rice cooker is easy – you can set the timer before you go to sleep, then in the morning you just need to add some milk and toppings and you are ready to eat. The best thing about porridge is that it's easily adapted to dietary requirements – like dairy-free, nut-free or vegan and with the abundance of frozen or fresh fruit available, it's a cheap and filling way to start your day.

HANDY TIP! Steel cut oats are our preferred type of oats to cook in a rice cooker. Rolled oats can be cooked, but can be a little tasteless – steel cut oats due to being less processed, require a longer cooking time and retain their texture when cooked.

COCOA, PEANUT BUTTER, RASPBERRIES

Add 1 tbsp of cocoa to the oats and water in the inner bowl before cooking. Once cooked, add a pinch of salt, loosen the porridge with any type of milk (cow, soy, coconut, oat), add a spoonful of peanut butter. Stir well so it's mixed right through the porridge. Taste and add honey, syrup or brown sugar if you needed. Spoon into bowls and top with raspberries (fresh or frozen).

APPLE, APRICOT AND PUMPKIN SEEDS

When the porridge is ready add a pinch of salt, loosen the with any type of milk (cow, soy, coconut, oat). Taste and add honey, syrup or brown sugar if you need it a little sweeter and stir through 1 tsp of cinnamon. Spoon into bowls and top with 30g dried apricots, 1 chopped red apple and 1 tsp pumpkin seeds.

PEAR AND CINAMMON

To the cooked porridge add a pinch of salt, loosen with any type of milk (cow, soy, coconut, oat). Taste and add honey, syrup or brown sugar if you need it a little sweeter and stir through 1 tsp of cinnamon. Spoon into bowls and top with sliced pears. (consider peach and raspberry as an alternative)

APPLE, MAPLE SYRUP AND PECAN

Once the cooking has finished, loosen the porrige with any type of milk (cow, soy, coconut, oat). Add maple syrup and stir until it's mixed through the porridge. Spoon into bowls and top with finely sliced apple and pecan nuts (whole or chopped)

YUMMY BANANA

Once the porridge has finished cooking, add a pinch of salt, loosen the porridge with any type of milk (cow, soy, coconut, oat), add a spoonful of peanut butter and stir well so it's mixed right thoroughly. Taste and add honey, syrup/brown sugar if you need it sweeter. Spoon into bowls and top with banana slices, drizzle with peanut butter and honey if you want a treat.

SWEET CARROT

At the end of porridge cooking add a pinch of salt and loosen the porridge with any type of milk (cow, soy, coconut, oat), add ⅓ a grated carrot, 1 tbsp of raisins,¼ tsp of cinnamon and a pinch of nutmeg. Stir well to make sure the mixture is distributed throughout and adjust the sweetness (optional) by adding honey, syrup or brown sugar. Spoon into bowls and top with more grated carrot, raisins and brown sugar (optional).

TOTALLY TROPICAL

When the porridge has finished, add a pinch of salt, loosen the porridge with coconut milk. Add honey/syrup/brown sugar (don't add too much at this point because the fruit will automatically sweeten the porridge). Spoon into bowls and top with orange slices/chunks, mango slices/chunks, banana slices, shredded or dessicated coconut, extra coconut milk and brown sugar.

CHOCOLATE ORANGE

Add 1 tbsp of cocoa to the oats and water in the inner bowl before the cooking. Once cooked add a pinch of salt, loosen the porridge with any type of milk (cow, soy, coconut, oat). Taste and add honey, syrup or brown sugar if you need it a little sweeter. Spoon into bowls and top with orange slices.

RICE GRAINS GUIDE

GET INTO THE GRAIN OF IT

Knowing the rice is to become the rice

Everyone at Yum Asia loves rice, and chances are, you do too. It can be a perfect side dish to so many things, but can also be the base of a full meal. You can flavour it in an almost infinite number of ways, or enjoy its inherent grainy perfume. However, there are numerous types of rice to start with, and staring down bags and boxes of white, brown, jasmine, basmati, sticky, and so on can be overwhelming. So we have created this guide about the different kinds of rice and how they can be cooked in our rice cookers.

Rice is a daily staple for nearly half of the world's 7.8 billion people according to the International Rice Research Institute. The majority of it is consumed in Asia but it is now strongly trending upwards in other countries, including the UK, Europe and the U.S. It's gluten-free (yes, even 'glutinous' rice) and simple to cook if you know the basic varieties and have a good quality rice cooker in your kitchen. So refer to the following section - go ahead and eat more rice because, let's face it, 3 billion people can't be wrong!

We first look at the **four characteristics of rice** that help you see just how varied rice can be and then we have a **guide to the different types of rice and their uses**. We then move to a guide to what you should look for when **choosing a rice cooker** which is followed by **tips** and **troubleshooting** rice cooker issues.

1. LENGTH AND SHAPE

Short, medium and long

Rice is characterised as one of three varieties - long grain, medium grain, or short grain rice.

These varieties refer to the length and shape of the grain. Simply speaking, long grain rice will have a longer cylindrical shape, whereas short grain rice will be shorter and wider.

Long Grain Rice - this rice has milled grains that are at least three to four times as long as they are wide. Due to it's starch composition, it is separate, light and fluffy when cooked.

Medium Grain rice - when compared to long grain rice, medium grain rice has a shorter, wider kernel. Since the cooked grains are more moist and tender than long grain rice, the rice has a tendency to stick together.

Short Grain Rice - featuring grains that are less than twice as long as they are wide, this rice is short and best fo sushi. It has a sticky texture when cooked.

2. COLOUR

Rice isn't always white

Rice is naturally brown after harvesting, but once the nutrient-rich outer layer of bran is removed, it is white in colour. Red, black and purple rice all feature unique pigment in the bran. For these rice varieties, the bran layer usually remains for added visual appeal and added nutritional value.

Polished Rice - the term 'polished' simply is white rice that has had its outer brown layer of bran and germ removed. It can also be referred to as 'milled rice'.

Brown Rice - this rice sheds its outer husk and retains its bran and germ layers that give it a characteristic brown colour. Takes longer to cook but is substantially more nutrient dense.

Forbidden Rice - high in nutritional value. Also known as black rice and has a mild nutty flavor. Used in many Chinese or Thai dishes, including black rice cake and mango sticky rice. Can also be used to add colour.

Wild Rice - harvested from the genus Zizania of grasses. High in protein, wild rice adds a colourful, exotic flair to any rice dish. Serve it with stir frys, soups or casseroles for a change.

3. AROMA

The sweet smell of rice

Aroma is another factor to consider when cooking with rice. Certain rice varieties give off pleasing fragrances while being cooked. Add a sensory element to your guests dining experience with these rice types.

Basmati rice - a long-grain rice that is popular among Indian cuisine and Middle Eastern dishes. Cooked basmati rice imparts a subtle nutty or popcorn-like flavour and aroma.

Jasmine rice - sometimes known as Thai fragrant rice, is a type of long grain rice with a long kernel and slightly sticky texture when cooked. Use it to infuse a subtle jasmine flavour and aroma into your dishes

IMPORTANT - easy cook or parboiled

Parboiled rice (also called converted rice and easy cook rice) is rice that has been partially boiled in the husk and is NOT suitable for use in fuzzy logic rice cookers. As this rice is already partly cooked (and not pure uncooked raw grains) it does not work well. This type of rice should only be used for rapid boiling or microwave cooking which, in our opinion, destroys the characteristics of rice that makes it so naturally tasty!

4. TEXTURE

Sticky or light and fluffy?

When cooking rice dishes, you'll want to think about the desired texture of the rice. The starch content varies from rice type to rice type and it will affect whether rice is sticky or light and fluffy.

Sticky rice - also known as sweet rice, it is grown mainly in South-East Asia. Used in many traditional Asian dishes, desserts, and sweets. When cooked, sticky rice is especially sticky and is often ground into rice flour.

Parboiled rice - this 'rough' rice has gone through a steam-pressure process before milling that gelatinises the starch in the grain. It is a more separate grain that is light and fluffy when cooked but with less taste.

Converted rice is a type of parboiled rice that has been further pre-cooked. This allows you to make dishes of rice even faster but **should never be used in a rice cooker!!**

Jasmine rice - predominantly from Thailand, it has long, translucent grains. When cooked, it has a seductive, slightly floral aroma and a soft, clingy texture. We recommend Hom Mali variety for best results.

Ideal for - curry, stir-fry dishes and other Thai and Asian cuisine

Rice cooker setting - LONG GRAIN, WHITE RICE, REGULAR or YUMAMI

Basmati rice -the predominant rice in Indian and Pakistani cuisine, is marked by it's extra long grains and a subtle nutty fragrance and flavour. Better if aged. Results can greatly vary depending on the variety. We recommend Super Kernel.

Ideal for - dal, curries, pilau or saffron rice. Pairs well with South Asian dishes.

Rice cooker setting - LONG GRAIN, WHITE RICE, REGULAR or YUMAMI

Standard long grain - American style white rice is the most familiar rice in western kitchens. During cooking, water gets completely absorbed by the rice for a dry, fluffy texture with distinct grains.

Often has less taste, texture and aroma.

Ideal for - general purpose dishes or food that requires blank canvas rice

Rice cooker setting - LONG GRAIN, WHITE RICE, REGULAR or YUMAMI

THE LONG GRAINS

Standard brown - American type brown rice is the whole-grain version of its white counterpart – that is to say, the bran and germ layers are left intact, giving the rice a nutty, grainy flavour and a chewy bite.

Ideal for - general purpose dishes or food that requires blank but nutty canvas of rice

Rice cooker setting - BROWN RICE OR GABA

THE MEDIUM AND SHORT GRAINS

Arborio rice - the most widely available variety of Italian superfino rice, used to make risotto (the other types include carnaroli and vialone nano). Plump grains, high proportion of amylopectin, a type of sticky starch that's responsible for the trademark creamy texture of risotto.

Ideal for - risotto, rice pudding

Rice cooker setting - SHORT GRAIN
(or WHITE SETTING if no short grain)

Short grain brown - like other short grain varieties, has a higher level of amylopectin, making it slightly sticky. The intact bran gives it more chew than white short grain rice.

Ideal for - healthier versions of sushi and risotto

Rice cooker setting - BROWN RICE or GABA

Japanese sushi rice - best for sushi, but also served plain as a finish to a typical meal. It's slightly translucent when raw, and firm but a bit sticky when cooked (but don't confuse it with Japanese sticky rice, used for the sweets called mochi).

Ideal for - sushi, seafood, Japanese dishes

Rice cooker setting - SHORT GRAIN
(or WHITE SETTING if no short grain)

Bomba rice - the rice of choice for the Spanish classic paella. It absorbs up to twice as much liquid as long-grain rice, but without getting sticky, like short-grain rice.

Ideal for - pairs well with Spanish dishes

Rice cooker setting - SHORT GRAIN
(or WHITE SETTING if no short grain)

Wehani rice - a whole-grain, reddish brown American hybrid of basmati and long grain brown rice. It's intense chew and deep colour make it popular for mixing with other rices in a pilaf.

Ideal for - pilaf, rice mixing for colour

Rice cooker setting - BROWN RICE or GABA

Kalijira rice - a medium-grain rice from the Bengal region of India, often called 'baby basmati' because of its diminutive size. It makes an intriguing alternative to basmati in a pilaf.

Ideal for - pilaf, Indian dishes

Rice cooker setting - SHORT GRAIN
(or WHITE SETTING if no short grain)

Wild rice - not a true rice but the seed of a grass native to North America. Most 'wild' rice sold in supermarkets today is actually cultivated. Deeply chewy, and adds interest to pilafs and plain rice.

Ideal for - dressings, casseroles, soups, salads, and desserts.

Rice cooker setting - BROWN RICE or GABA

Chinese black rice - also known as forbidden rice. A whole-grain rice that cooks firm, non-sticky, and tender. It's dramatic colour (deep purple when cooked) makes it a particularly striking rice.

Ideal for - porridge, dessert, traditional Chinese black rice cake

Rice cooker setting - BROWN RICE or GABA

Glutinous rice - glue-like or sticky, and not in the sense of containing gluten (which it does not). Often called 'sticky', rice can be short or long grain

Ideal for - desserts, mango sticky rice and Asian dishes

Rice cooker setting - SHORT or LONG GRAIN

Thai riceberry - entered the rice market over ten years ago and is well known for its unique appearance, nutritional value and health benefits. Can be mixed with white jasmine for a fun blend.

Ideal for - high nutrition, very healthy, Thai dishes

Rice cooker setting - BROWN or GABA

THE OTHERS

Whilst not strictly grains, rice cookers are very good at cooking the following seeds/pulses/legumes. This is because of the way that rice cookers heat and cook.

You just need to experiment with adjusting water levels and selecting the correct cooking cycle. They are largely good as a subsitute for rice and are extremely healthy for your body.

Quinoa- resembles a whole-grain but is actually a seed. Described as a superfood it's an excellent plant based source of protein, fibre, antioxidants and a range of minerals.

Ideal for - use as a subsitute for rice

Rice cooker setting - QUICK COOK/WHITE

Cous Cous - tiny granules made from steamed and dried durum wheat it has a light fluffy texture, mild in flavour but readily soaks up the flavours of other ingredients.

Ideal for - Moroccan/Middle Eastern dishes

Rice cooker setting - QUICK COOK/WHITE

Millet - like quinoa it is actually a seed and not a grain. It can be said to be like a mini fluffy corn with a slightly nutty flavour.
Can take on characteristics of it's paired meal and be a susbstitute for rice.

Ideal for - use instead of rice or oats

Rice cooker setting - PORRIDGE

Lentils and beans - both legumes are often catagorised by their colour and shape.

Some are better for certain dishes than others such as red lentils for dal or kidney beans for chilli.

Ideal for - lentils great for dal and other Asian, African dishes. Beans are versatile

Rice cooker setting - SLOW COOK/PORRIDGE

Pearl barley - similar to brown rice in health benefits but it has gluten. It's a great source of fibre, vitamins and minerals. It has a popular taste and is one of the more versatile grains.

Ideal for - best for soups, salads, stews

Rice cooker setting - SLOW COOK

RICE IS HEALTHY
An incredible source of nutrition

RICE is one of the oldest cultivated crops, first mentioned in history as far back as 2800 BC in China. Rice is a staple crop and forms the foundation of the diet for many of the world's population, especially those living in South and Eastern Asia. There are four major categories of rice worldwide - indica, japonica, aromatic and glutinous and it's thought there are over 140,000 different varieties of rice, but only a few varieties are grown widely. In many Asian languages the word for rice is interchangeable with the word for food and is the staple food of over half the world's population.

THE SCIENCE - Rice is an excellent source of energy. It is comprised of 77.5% carbohydrate which is one of the body's two main sources of energy, the second being fat. Like other cereals, the carbohydrate in rice is mainly in the form of starch - a complex carbohydrate, and like other cereals the starches occur in granules in the endosperm.

Starch exists as either amylose or amylopectin and comprises units of glucose (a simple sugar) linked together in very large numbers. During digestion, the links are broken and the resulting glucose is absorbed into the body. Amylopectin contains branches and is less resistant to digestion whereas amylose is a straight chain molecule and harder for the digestive system to break up. This means that rice varieties with a greater proportion of starch in the form of amylose tend to have a lower glycaemic index.

· Rice is low in fat/cholesterol and high in starchy carbohydrates.
· Rice is packed full of vitamins and minerals and provides an excellent source of vitamin E, B vitamins (thiamin, niacin) and potassium which helps the body fight toxins.
· Brown rice and basmati rice have medium or low GI values, and aren't associated with risk factors for weight gain and diabetes.
· Rice is very easy to digest meaning no unwanted discomfort.
· It is low in fat, low in cholesterol, high in starch.
· Rice can contribute significantly to vitamin and mineral intake, although the contribution to micronutrient intake will depend on the proportion of germ, bran and endosperm consumed (i.e. the balance between brown and white rice).
· It's recommended that 33% of meals are based on carbohydrate rich food such as rice.
· Allergic reactions to rice are rare.

Tasty and full of vitamins
WHY IS RICE GOOD FOR YOU?

NOT ALL COOKED RICE IS THE SAME

- Rice is cooked by boiling or steaming, and it absorbs water during cooking – so much water is absorbed, it triples in size!

- Rice (or any other grain) is sometimes quickly fried in oil or fat before boiling (for example, saffron rice or risotto); this makes the cooked rice less sticky. This cooking style is commonly called pilaf by American chefs or biryani (dam-pukhtak) in India, Pakistan and Iran.

- In Middle Eastern cuisine, rice is an ingredient of many soups and dishes with fish, poultry and other types of meat. It is also used to stuff vegetables or is wrapped in grape leaves (dolma).

- When combined with milk, sugar, and honey, it is used to make desserts. In some regions, bread is made using rice flour. Medieval Islamic texts spoke of medical uses for the rice plant.

- Rice may also be made into congee (also called rice porridge, fawrclaab, okayu, Xifan, jook, or rice gruel) by adding more water than usual, so that the cooked rice is saturated with water, usually to the point that it disintegrates. Rice porridge is commonly eaten as a breakfast food, and is also a traditional food for the sick.

- Rice may be soaked prior to cooking, which saves fuel, decreses cooking time, minimises exposure to high temperature and thus decreases the stickiness of the rice. For some varieties, soaking improves the texture of the cooked rice by increasing expansion of the grains. By using a fuzzy logic rice cooker you will never have to soak the rice.

- By far the easiest way of cooking rice is in a rice cooker. Several models of rice cookers use fuzzy logic technology which make cooking rice very simple. However, rather than simply boiling the rice, these rice cookers use multiple heat application phases (steam, boil, braise) and make small adjustments to the temperature to produce rice which is perfect!

Food can be classified according to their glycaemic index (GI). The GI is intended to measure how quickly a carbohydrate food is absorbed into the blood stream. Foods with a higher GI are, in principle, more quickly digested than those with a lower GI value.

Eating low GI foods like rice means that the energy released from the food is slower and therefore keeps you feeling fuller for longer!

To simplify things, the rate of digestion and absorption is influenced by a number of factors:

GLYCAEMIC INDEX AND IT'S MEANING

- Cooking method and amount of chewing (the more food is chewed, the higher the value)
- Cooking or processing (milling increases the GI)
- The nature and amount of carbohydrate
- Other food components (presence of fat and protein tends to lower GI values)
- The nature of the starch (ratio of amylose to amylopectin)
- Individual variation. Given the same food, there can be a 50% variation in GI value between individuals

Brown rice can be germinated in order to alter the flavour and also increase levels of nutrients such as gamma-aminobutyric acid (GABA). This rice has a softer texture than brown rice, a nuttier flavour and a lower GI value.

Scientific studies have shown that a germinated brown rice rich diet can improve cognitive function and other studies have found that it can act as an anti-diabetic.

THAT'S A LOT OF RICE
The average person in much of Asia eats rice two or three times a day. The average person in Myanmar eats 195kg of rice each year; in Lao PDR and Cambodia, it's about 160kg. Contrast this with the average European, who consumes 3kg per year and the average American, who eats 7kg.

MUD, SWEAT, AND GAZING AT A WATER BUFFALO'S REAR END
To plow 1 ha of rice land in the traditional way, a farmer and his water buffalo (preparing land is almost always men's work) must walk 80 km.

WHAT? WILD RICE ISN'T RICE?
So-called 'wild rice' isn't rice at all - it's actually a grass!

GROW IT, EAT IT
Most rice is consumed in the country where it is produced. Only 5 percent of the world's total is exported. Thailand ships the most: between 5-7 million tonnes a year. The USA is second with nearly 3 million tonnes, and Vietnam third, with 2 million tonnes.

AN OLD OLD CROP
It is generally believed that human beings have been growing rice for over 5000 years.

HEALTH BENEFITS
Rice can reduce heart disease and certain cancers and is helpful for the gut.

RICE FACTS

THIRSTY RICE
It takes 5,000 litres of water to produce one kilogram of rice.

WHY IS MY BACK SORE?
In Asia, planting rice is often a back-breaking chore. Every seedling must be poked into the mud by hand usually by women.

HIGH-TECH RICE PRODUCTION
Many rice farmers in the United States level their fields with laser controlled earthmovers and seed their fields from airplanes.

THAT'S DIVERSITY!
More than 140,000 varieties of cultivated rice (the grass species Oryza Sativa) are thought to exist - but no one really knows for sure. More than 90,000 samples of cultivated rice and wild species are stored in trust in the International Rice Genebank for use by researchers around the world.

RICE-EATING COUNTRIES
Three of the world's four most populous nations are rice based societies - China, India, and Indonesia. Together, they have nearly 3 billion people.

AN ASIAN CROP
Most rice in the world is grown in East and Southeast Asia, with China and India producing the most.

THE GREAT WALL OF CHINA IS HELD TOGETHER BY STICKY RICE
While the Great Wall was being built during the Ming dynasty in the 15th and 16th centuries, workers used a porridge made with rice along with calcium carbonate as a mortar to hold the wall's stones together.

RICE CAN'T GET ANY GREATER THAN THIS!

RICE COOKERS EXPLAINED

THE ORIGIN OF THE RICE COOKER

Have you ever wondered how the idea of the electric rice cooker began? If you like rice and enjoy the benefits of rice cookers as much as we do then you will find the following few pages fascinating.

Let's face it, cooking on a stove can be very troublesome. If you don't time or measure things correctly you can end up with mush or a complete mess of a stove. Viral videos are all over the internet showing how bad people are at cooking rice in a saucepan with 'World War Two is over, use technology!' being the thrust of the message. The 'automatic rice cooker' is a mid 20th century invention that made the culinary labour intensive task of hovering over a stove as easy as measuring rice and water in a rice cooker and pressing a button. They can be super smart too and are almost impossible to mess things up. However, the creation of these wonderous kitchen appliances was not easy. It took determination and some significant inventive leaps by even the biggest of names in Japanese technology. Let's dig a little deeper into how the rice cooker idea began and became perfected.

The Kamado

The ancient way of cooking rice in Japan was to use a **Kamado**. This is a box shaped cooker range topped with a heavy cast iron pot. This traditional method of rice cooking was incredibly tricky. A careful combination of increased heat and less heat was used to cook the rice but doing this with a wood fire was an almost impossible task. Every day, Japanese women would spend hours sweating over the Kamado to make rice. This often involved waking at dawn and bellowing the flames for 15 minutes before they could even think about getting the rice cooking. It could take hours and was extremely labourious.

The early attempts of Ibuka

The birth of the rice cooker happened around the year 1923. A company called 'Mitsubishi Electric' released a very basic industrial model. About 10 years later the Japanese even deployed a multi cooker in the war but rice cookers for the household were still decades away. It was an uphill struggle because with Japanese rice some starch has to be converted to sugar so that it has a sweet taste with a sticky texture, separate grains and the correct moisture. It wasn't just a process of boiling the rice grains with high heat only. Japanese people were incredibly picky about their rice and finding an automated way to make the perfect rice was still only a dream.

In 1945 war-torn Japan faced an uphill struggle of rehabilitation and rebuilding when an engineer called **Masaru Ibuka** opened a radio workshop. He chose an abandoned telephone switchboard room in a vacant department store as his new headquarters. A year later Ibuka wrote down the words that would later become iconic to the company that in 1958 would become known as Sony: "Purpose of incorporation: Creating an ideal workplace, free, dynamic, joyous."

As his company grew, Ibuka's engineers received payment of uncooked rice in part payment of their fixing radios. This resulted in the companies first invention. No, not a radio – but instead an electric rice cooker. It was crude but effective resembling a rustic wooden tub with aluminium filaments (see image left). It was an ingenious idea! The rice itself would function as the timer switch, as the water evaporated and the rice dried it would theoretically break the connection with the filament and turn off the cooker.

Whilst the future for post-war Japan was getting brighter, fuel remained expensive but electricity was relatively cheap and plentiful. Ibuka bought a whole container of wooden tubs and started to turn them into electric rice cookers with the help of a friend who supplied black market rice to help test them.

However, Ibuku claimed that unless the rice was of a good consistent quality there would be a problem as poor quality rice would absorb water incorrectly and make it mushy or too dry, flaky or broken. The warehouse of Ibuka was filled with wooden tubs and Ibuka lost hope of making the perfect rice cooker and went back to fixing radios. Sony never returned to making rice cookers but their corporate museum in Shinagawa still have one of the rustic wooden bucket rice cooker prototypes. Sony's attempt into the rice cooker evolution was fleeting but gave ideas to other Japanese electronics companies at the time. Many released electricity powered rice cookers but they were not automatic – having to be constantly monitored.

The struggle to make a working automatic rice cooker

The struggle continued until a salesman called **Shogo Yamada** working for Toshiba, promoting the company's first electric washing machine, made it a success. Going from Japanese kitchen to kitchen he often asked housewives about their most laborious task. Their answer was nearly always about the daily cooking of rice (up to 3 times a day) which at that time was still often performed using a kamado.

A very fortuitous chance meeting then happened between Yamada and **Yoshitada Minami** who came looking for work with Yamada. With his background in making water heaters (unsucessfully) Minami was tasked by Yamada to come up with a rice cooking machine Since cooking rice was largely a woman's task back then, he passed much of the research for this project to his wife, **Fumiko**.

The invention of a rice cooker at Toshiba wasn't given priority because Yamada's supervisors had seen Mitsubishi and Matushita (what would eventually become Panasonic) fail at creating an automatic electric washing machine. They also believed that any woman that gave up the time, effort and the sleep it took to make perfect rice was a 'failed houswife'.

Minami had the engineering knowledge to make an automated electric rice cooker work but his wife knew how to cook the rice perfectly and did that on a traditional kamado everyday to feed their six children. To support the project, Minami took out a loan using their family home as collateral while Fumiko studied the existing rice cookers on the market.

The idea of the rice cooker they came up with was that when water in a pot of rice has been totally absorbed or evaporated away, the temperature of the container increases rapidly (since the temperature of liquid water generally can't exceed 100°C, but the temperature of rice certainly can), the magic to make this work automatically was a bimetallic strip provided by Yamada to Toshiba that would turn the rice cooker off by bending once the temperature in the pot exceeded 100°C.

Fumiko endlessly tested prototype after prototype, cooking rice on the roof, in the sun, in the cold, and in the heat. Preventing the pot from releasing heat during cooking was challenging. However, Yamada remembered that in Hokkaido state (where the winters are brutal) the cooking pots there were heavily insulated. Their final product therefore had a two layered wall. One inside and the other covered in three layers of iron. Toshiba's first automatic rice cooker, the **ER-4** was then ready for mass production (see image right).

The **Toshiba ER-4**, the companies first automated rice cooker

The early days of the Matsushita (Panasonic) company. The president (top left) **Konosuke Matsushita** pushed hard for rice cooker development

Getting the world to see the benefits of rice cookers...

These gadgets wouldn't come cheap however and many Japanese housewives were hesitant to buy one. Yamada went on the road to demonstrate the effectiveness of how the rice cooker not only prepared the rice but also how it could perfectly make takikomi gohan, a finicky rice dish with a soy-based sauce that often burned. The culinary masses got hooked and within the year, Toshiba was producing 200,000 rice cookers every month!

On the trail of Toshiba's success, the war of rice cooker manufcturing began. The next year, Matsushita Electric, now better known as Panasonic (see image left), jumped into the fight. The companies employees were horrified that Toshiba had beaten them with this miraculous gadget.

Matsushita was the most well known for it's household gadgets after all. It was therefore seen as a disgrace that such a convenient home appliance as the rice cooker should have come from Toshiba, a manufacturer that was better known for producing industrial machines.

How the rice cooker went global

Matsushita's president, **Konosuke Matsushita** gave one employee such a berating that colleagues feared he would commit suicide. That man was **Tatsunosuke Sakamoto** and he was very passionate about rice cookers. He had a dream of a market of international demand for such gadgets. To get ahead of the Toshiba competition, Matshushita needed to make a rice cooker with only one pot. This would use less metal and result in a cheaper device.

Matsushita released their **EC-36 rice cooker** (see image below), with its single pot in 1956. Then in 1959, Sakamoto, now head of the company's Rice Cooker Division, teamed up with William Mong, the Hong Kong-based distributor of Matsushita products. They modified the rice cooker for Hong Kong consumers and Matsushita learned how to adapt the rice cooker to international tastes before finally taking the gadget to Asia, the Middle East, and around the world.

An icon and a game changer

The electric automated rice cooker became so iconic that even the Smithsonian museum has a Matsushita rice cooker in it's collection. This was a simple on/off one button appliance with a basic keep warm function. By the 1970s such cookers were quickly adopted by older rice-centric communities in South Carolina and Louisiana and by newer counter-cultural Americans who were increasingly interested in alternate cuisines and culinary practices. In a way, it was the culmination of Sakamoto's dream.

Within a few years of the automated electric rice cooker's release, more than 50 percent of Japan's households had one. It completely revolutionised work in the kitchen and was the one household appliance that every household in Japan wanted.

The advertising for Toshiba's first rice cooker emphasised over and over that it would liberate women from standing or squatting at the kamado, constantly keeping an eye on the rice. Agreed, it did ease the laborious hovering over the kamado but didn't result in a win for women's liberation. However, it gave women more time to enter the workforce, do other household chores and spend time with their family. It was truly a revolution in a way.

The **Matsushita EC-36,** one pot rice cooker

Present day rice cookers

Nowadays the variety of automated electric rice cookers is large. Many rice cookers for the home use technology and inner bowl materials to recreate the flavour of kamado-cooked rice, which is still widely available in traditional restaurants. The type of cooking which involved changing temperatures in stages that was once laborious can now be done automatically.

Only the development of induction-heating cookers in the 1980's have allowed for the kind of instant high temperatures that a wood burning stove produces and the ability to agitate the rice like that of kamado operator.

For those not seeking the flavour of the kamado more basic rice cookers may be the best choice. Without any microcomputers or touchscreens, they still operate using a single button and a design that halts cooking once the container surpasses 100°C but they only boil the rice rather than modulate the cooking pot temperature varying the style of cooking like a kamado operator would do (steaming, boiling, braising etc).

The morale of this story is this, **'Perfection takes time'.**
To cook rice perfectly using a device that makes rice taste amazing like that from a kamado, it is probably worth investing in something a little bit more than a basic on/off button rice cooker.

CHOOSING A RICE COOKER
Steps to buying the perfect device

WHAT ARE MODERN RICE COOKERS?

Going way back in time, the very old way of cooking rice would be a fire with some kind of clay pot that would boil the rice. Until recently a similar method has been used except the fire has been replaced by a basic heating element and the clay pot has been replaced with a basic non stick inner bowl. These are what we call very basic rice cookers. They usually have a loose glass lid too and an on/off switch. The more premium rice cookers are a lot more advanced using a heating method that is not just a basic boil. Instead a clever brain (fuzzy logic) calculates the correct amount of heat and type of heat applied to the rice. There are sensors in the unit, timer functions and a whole range of other features that not only make your rice taste amazing with great texture but make everything easier and more versatile too!

OLD RICE COOKERS
Glass lid or jar type with simple on/off button

X Spit Starchy Water
No condensation collection

X Poor Inner Bowls
Basic non-stick bowl

X No Timers
No presetting/no keep warm

X No Fuzzy Logic
They operate like a pan

X Overly Wet Rice
Inaccurate water level balancing

X Boils Only
No phased cooking

X Hard To Clean
Parts don't come apart for easy access

PREMIUM RICE COOKERS
Usually computer controlled or similar

✓ No Water Spillage
Usually sealed units

✓ High Quality Inner Bowls
Durable materials (ceramic, Sumiflon)

✓ 24 Hour Timer Function
Preset turning on then keep warm at end

✓ Advanced Fuzzy Logic
Smart tech calculates time and heat

✓ Multi Phased Cooking
Not just boiling but steaming, braising...

✓ Modern Appearance
Latest LED displays and buttons

✓ Easy To Clean
Parts come apart and easy to clean

Typical Way A Premium Rice Cooker Works

1. MEASURE RICE - take your favourite brand of rice and measure how many cups of rice you want to make into your provided measuring cup

2. PUT IN INNER BOWL - rinse your rice (if needed) by putting the rice into a sieve and running water through it. Place the rice into the inner bowl of your rice cooker.

3. FILL BOWL WITH WATER - fill up the inner bowl of your rice cooker with water to the corresponding rice cup level line for the type of rice you are cooking. Depending on how sticky or dry you want your rice you can make small adjustments in water level at this stage.

4. CLOSE LID AND PRESS START - close the lid, select the function for your rice type on the display and press start. The rice cooker will then prepare delicious rice automatically and beep or play a tune to let you know when your rice is ready.

5. KEEP WARM - to keep your rice at the correct temperature the cooker will auto switch to keep warm in case you are running a bit late!

WHAT SIZE OF RICE COOKER DO YOU NEED?

1 cup
(1 Person)
0.18 Litre

2.5 cup
(1-2 People)
0.45 Litre

3.5 cup
(1-3 People)
0.6 Litre

5.5 cup
(1-5 People)
1 Litre

8 cup
(1-8 People)
1.5 Litre

10 cup
(1-10 People)
1.8 Litre

The first thing to consider is the size of the rice cooker you need. Rice cookers come in different sizes, these sizes are usually termed in rice measuring cup sizes or litre. The usual sizes are :

1 cup (0.18 litre), **2.5 cup** (0.45 litre), **3 cup** (0.5 litre), **4 cup** (0.7 litre), **5.5 cup** (1 litre), **8 cup** (1.5 litre) and **10 cup** (1.8 litre). All of these maximum capacities are for uncooked white rice, brown rice capacity is lower due to the fact it cooks/expands differently to white rice.

The cup size of a rice cooker roughly corresponds to how many people you are cooking for, however, it also depends on how much rice you usually cook per person (how much rice each person likes to eat).

So, the measuring cup provided with rice cookers is 180ml. These maximum capacities shown in this image should help you work out which rice cooker is the better option for you. The volumes show uncooked rice amounts. You also need to consider if you are going to be entertaining people or wanting to cook extra for lunches, if so, you should factor this into the size you need to use.

WHAT RICE COOKING FUNCTIONS DO YOU WANT?

It's always useful to know what functions you would like in a rice cooker. Some you may need more than others. Most rice cookers have functions in common. These are white rice, brown rice, sweet rice (for sticky/glutinous rice), quick cook, porridge, timer and keep warm. One thing to note is that not every model will have all of the features you want, so you may need to make a choice between what functions are most important for you.

White rice
This 'WHITE' function is usually referred to as long grain but can also refer to short grain depending on the rice cooker. Often rice cookers will distinguish between long and short grain by having individual functions for each rice type

Long grain white rice
Roughly four times as long as it is wide and includes varieties such as white basmati and jasmine rice. If your rice cooker doesn't have a 'LONG GRAIN' function, then 'WHITE' function should be used along with the water levels for 'white' on the inner bowl.

Short grain white rice
Short grain rice is short and plump and can include sushi rice, pearl rice and Thai sticky or glutinous rice. In rice cookers without a short grain setting, it should be cooked on the 'WHITE' function, however, some rice cookers have a dedicated 'SHORT GRAIN' function.

Brown rice
Like white rice this can also be short or long grain but the overriding factor is, that it's brown rice, so it needs more cooking no matter the length of the grain.

You should always use the 'BROWN' function on a rice cooker. The cooking cycles for brown rice do take longer – this is because of two factors, first there is more bran on the outside of the rice grain, so it takes longer to cook and second because there is more water involved during the cooking cycle and it takes longer to evaporate.

Black, red and Thai rice berry rice should also be cooked on the 'BROWN' rice function.

'Yumami'/'Premium Taste'
Some cookers have one of these functions which is for any type of white rice. It brings out the 'umami' taste. The rice is cooked in a different way (using a specially designed soaking and steaming cooking cycle) which makes the rice taste sweeter and moreish – it really makes a difference to the taste.

GABA brown
The 'GABA' function pre-soaks the rice at a specific temperature to sprout or 'activate' the rice. It's said to release GABA (gamma-aminobutyric acid).

YumCarb/Low Carb
The YumCarb or Low Carb function can be used for both white and brown rice. By cooking rice in the provided stainless steel steaming basket, the rice is cooked in a special way so that the sugars in the rice are not re-absorbed and results in the cooked rice being up to 25% lower in carb value.

Crust/Tahdig
Some rice cookers have a CRUST function which can be used to prepare crispy rice. In several countries crispy/crusty rice plays a big part in cuisine - in Korea it's called nurungji and family members often fight over it; in Iran it's called Tahdig and can be flavoured with different spices. The crust setting can also be used to make claypot rice in a pinch.

Claypot rice
Claypot rice, sometimes translated as "rice casserole", is a traditional dinner dish in Southern China and Southeast Asia, mainly Hong Kong, Malaysia and Singapore. Some rice cookers have a specific CLAYPOT function for the cooking of this rice.

WHAT ADD-ON FUNCTIONS DO YOU WANT?

As rice cookers are sealed units with a specific way of heating and controlling the retention or release of moisture they can also be very good at specific cooking functions other than rice.

Steam
Some rice cookers have a 'STEAM' function with steaming baskets included. This is very useful for creating full meals in the one appliance, you can steam vegetables, meat, fish, dumplings while you are cooking rice. You can even use the steam setting as a stand-alone steamer.

Cake baking
Yes! rice cookers can bake too. Usually the function is labelled 'CAKE' or 'BAKE'. If you like fantastic moist cakes, cheesecake, banana cake, brownies, spiced apple cake – all are amazing because the cakes are steamed rather than baked. For some delicious recipes, see our dessert section!

Porridge
For oatmeal or traditional rice porridge (known as congee) look for the 'PORRIDGE' function. There is nothing better than using a rice cooker to have your porridge ready for breakfast on a cold winter day.

Slow Cook
Some (but not many) rice cookers have a 'SLOW COOK' function. The very best cookers with this setting will allow you to set the time of the cooking cycle.

Soup
Make anything from vegetable to meat soups with the 'SOUP' function if your rice cooker has this.

Yoghurt
As rice cookers can keep temperatures stable and contents in an incubation state, this makes certain rice cookers ideal for making 'YOGHURT'.

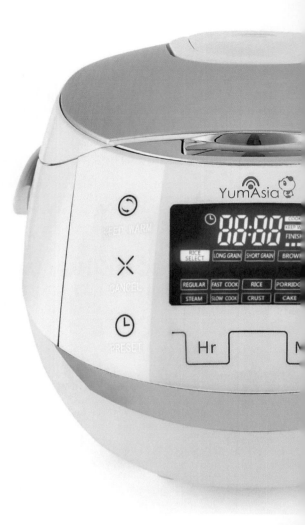

WHAT TYPE OF INNER BOWL?

Of increasing importance to many people is the type of material the inner bowl is made from. The main types are teflon like non-stick coated bowls, ceramic coated bowls, pure ceramic bowls, stainless steel/glass bowls.

Glass and steel do not generally fit well with rice cooking. Rice sticks to steel like glue and glass at high temperatures can become fragile. Our advice is to use a ceramic based bowl if possible. As a second choice a good non stick Teflon like coated bowl is also okay provided it is hard wearing.

Also consider the thickness of the bowl. Thicker is often better as the heat can be more evenly distributed. If the bowl has multiple layers then usually these bowls are constructed to conduct heat at the correct rate whilst giving a healthy type of protection on the food contact layer.

CONVENTIONAL HEATING OR INDUCTION HEATING (IH)?

Induction Heating (IH) is more expensive but gives more even heating and unique rice functions.

More advanced conventional heating rice cookers can have 3D technology to spread the heat around the bowl more evenly.

Conventional Heating

The majority of rice cookers available are basic conventional on/off with a loose fitting glass lid (during cooking starchy water can spit out) or are a basic jar type of rice cooker. These rice cookers are only marginally better than using a saucepan – they simply boil the rice, reacting to when a certain temperature is reached, it switches off. A lot of these types of rice cookers burn the rice or over-cook it.

The more premium, conventionally heated rice cookers are completely sealed units, so no mess is created when cooking. Often they will have some type of fuzzy logic technology. This means that whilst the rice is cooking the brain of the cooker is constantly adjusting the temperature, cooking time and type of heat applied to give perfect rice. Fuzzy logic calculates the temperatures and reacts, making the heating element react to different stages of the cooking cycle. The rice is cooked using many different types of heat cycles (phased cooking) rather than boiled and the resulting rice is far better in taste, aroma and texture.

Induction Heating (IH)

The other type of rice cooker is Induction Heating (IH). This method of heating uses coils in the bottom of the cooker to create a magnetic field. When the stainless steel inductive layer of the non-stick ceramic inner cooking bowl is placed into the rice cooker and the unit is activated, the magnetic field generated creates instant heat throughout this layer.

This technology enables the inner cooking pan itself rather than the heating element to become the heat source. This means that you can get a high heat which is more evenly distributed and the cooker can make fine heat adjustments to control the cooking process.

Exclusive to Yum Asia's IH rice cooker models is **UMAI** Induction Heating (IH). 'Umai' in Japanese means smart brain which refers to the microprocessor used to make fine adjustments in temperature and cooking times (phased cooking). The **UMAI** IH sytem is so smart (by combining the latest IH coil technology with advanced fuzzy logic), it makes the rice cooker more efficient, this means your rice is absolutely perfect every single time and it is cooked faster than other IH rice cookers.

Please note that you should be careful when buying IH models for your location. As these types of rice cookers use strong magnets and very specific electrical requirements they have to be fully compliant with safety directives for where you live. Buying from overseas markets may seem okay until you find out that they are not compatible or cannot be legally used in your home.

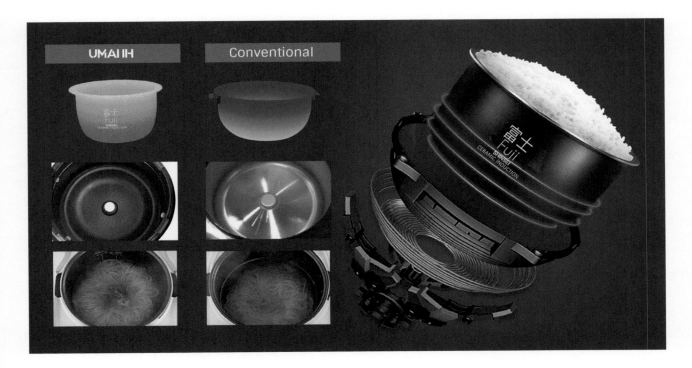

DISPLAYS AND COUNTDOWNS

Liquid Crystal Displays (LCD)
These type of displays were used in 1980s rice cookers until present day (the type of display found in calculators and Casio watches). Consume little power, are versatile but unstable and cannot be viewed in dark rooms.

Light Emitting Diode Displays (LED)
LED displays became popular in kitchen appliances in the late 1990s after the technology was perfected. More functionality and easier to use in your kitchen no matter how dark or bright and importantly with very good energy efficiency.

Rice Cookers With No Countdown
Some rice cookers with LCD or LED displays may not have any type of countdown. They may just have a progress bar which shows the cooking duration. Given that most rice cookers now have a keep warm function, if you are not concerned with having your rice 'just finished' then a cooker without a countdown indicator may be okay for you.

Rice Cookers With Last 10 Minute Countdown
The majority of modern day rice cookers have some kind of countdown which appears when the last 10 minutes of cooking occurs. This type of countdown is used in models by most major manufacturers due to high accuracy.

The reason why the remaining duration of time to cooking completed is not displayed until the final 10 minutes is because the fuzzy logic processor in the cooker needs to time to first calculate various cooking factors. These factors include ambient room temperature, starting bowl water temperature, the type of rice being cooked, the function chosen and other factors.

Most rice cookers can then only accurately determine the final 10 minutes and start counting down as they take time to work out the time to complete cooking.

Rice Cookers With A Full Countdown
Some rice cookers attempt to show a full countdown during the rice cooking process. Normally this type of countdown is inaccurate and the countdown jumps around until the final stages of cooking as the fuzzy logic works out how much more cooking time is required based on the conditions of the cooking. So actually only the last 10 minutes or so is usually accurate as an indicator of remaining cooking time. Some more advanced models employ a combination of 'smarter brain' processing such as Yum Asia's **UMAI** IH technology which can more accurately determine the remaining cooking time.

APPEARANCE AND OTHER FACTORS

Appearance
Rice cookers come in different colours, finishes, materials and vary in shape and syle. Think about if you want a metallic or glossy effect finish or a mixture of both. Do you want to go for minimalist or do you want to make a statement in your kitchen! Would you prefer the kawaii (cute) look or a more sleek appearance?

Hygiene, health and cleaning
Certain models have features that make them easier to maintain and clean. These can include condensation collectors, removable inner lids and steam caps (where steam vents out of) for easy cleaning. Think about how easy it is to keep those control panels clean, some of which are touch sensitive for better hygiene. Also some models have carry handles that help to move them around the kitchen or you prefer to easily hide them out of sight.

Spare Parts
Make sure that the brand you choose can supply spare parts for your rice cooker. You want it to last as long as possible after all. The most common part of a rice cooker that eventually may need replacing is the inner bowl and inner lid so check for those spares. Some people even prefer to have a spare inner bowl for convenience.

RICE COOKER PROBLEM TROUBLESHOOTER

My cooked rice is too hard or soft
- Make sure your rice cooker is on a flat surface.
- Remember that using the timer results in softer rice.
- Remember that using the QUICK COOK function usually results in slightly harder rice.
- Add more water (if rice is too hard) or less water (if rice is too soft) next time you cook the rice. Small water adjustments can make a large difference in the final rice texture.

The rice is scorched
- Check nothing is stuck on the underside of the inner bowl or on the heating element.
- The rice may not have been rinsed properly so there is too much starch left on the rice.
- Consider adding slightly more water before starting the cooking cycle. Too little water can cause the rice to scorch.

Why is the water boiling over during cooking?
- Check the inner lid is attached properly.
- The rice may not have been rinsed properly so there is too much starch left on the rice.
- Check to see if you added too much water.
- Check you are cooking within the maximum capacity of the rice cooker and remember that the maximum capacity is different for white and brown rice.

The timer can't be set
- Remember to press the start/cooking button after you have set the timer.
- You may need to press the start/cooking button to complete setting the timer.

Why is there a funny smell or the rice is yellow/too dry?
- Make sure the bowl is properly cleaned after using it for mixed rice or other dishes.
- Don't keep the rice warm for over 12 hours (Zojirushi) or keep too little rice on the KEEP WARM function.
- Don't keep the rice warm with the spatula inside the inner bowl.
- Loosen the rice after cooking is completed, stirring it thoroughly.
- If using the KEEP WARM function we find that the rice can deteriorate after 12 hours of use of this function. To keep the rice moist we recommend you periodically add splashes of water and mix through the rice. This prevents the rice drying out.
- Remember that the KEEP WARM function keeps the rice at a fairly high temperature still. This is for food safety but it also means that some of the water will evaporate from the rice. Using KEEP WARM often results in drier rice. Use the tip above to help mitigate this.

NOTE - All newly bought kitchen appliances will have some type of smell for the first few uses. Some people say that they smell new, of plastic or similar aroma. Please do not be alarmed. This is why we suggest to run a rice cooking cycle through the cooker first and throw away the rice as it will help remove any manufacturing residual aromas.

The rice cooker doesn't cook
- Check it's plugged in. If it is plugged in, check the power cord is pushed firmly into the unit. It only takes a little bit of the connector to not be in contact to cause the rice cooker not to work correctly.
- Make sure 'KEEP WARM' function isn't on, if so press CANCEL or RESET and then the START/ COOKING button

I have a strange white film on the inner bowl when the rice is cooked!
- This happens when the rice has a lot of starch. You should try rinsing/washing the rice more to remove it or buy less starchy rice.

The rice cooker started cooking immediately after the timer was set
- Check the timer is set correctly. If the timer is set to a shorter time than the default cooking programme's time then the rice cooker will start cooking immediately.

The rice is not ready at the correct time
- Check the timer is set correctly. Timers on rice cookers are rarely *exact*. The timer will switch the rice cookers on slightly earlier as the fuzzy logic has to figure out what exactly is in the inner bowl (rice/oats/ water) and volume so it can calculate the cooking time effectively. It deals with this by turning the unit on early so it can 'assess' the contents. The completed cooking time and length of cooking time will be the same as if you didn't use the timer, but there is some **figuring out time** built into the timer feature so you may see a discrepancy with the keep warm time displayed – it's normal.

RICE COOKER HELPFUL TIPS

Premium rice cookers can do a lot of the thinking for you but certain tweaks can make the rice you cook absolutely perfect. After all, not everyone likes their rice the same. Some people like rice to stick together whilst some prefer more individual grains and you can do a few simple things to achieve rice cooking perfection.

Buy the very best rice you can
- We usually use super kernel basmati and Thai Hom Mali jasmine rice for our plain white rice. For Japanese dishes we only use high quality short grains from Japan itself.
- When choosing packs of rice, make sure there aren't too many broken grains in there as this can sometimes cause a problem with rice being sticky, stodgy or mushy - make sure the majority of the grains are unbroken. Buying a decent sized pillow type bag at least 5kg in size will help reduce broken grain issues.
- Read the packet carefully to ensure the rice isn't any kind of quick cook or partially cooked rice (a giveaway is a cooking time of 10-12 mins). This type of rice is absolutely **not suitable** for using in your fuzzy logic rice cooker.

Measure and rinse your rice correctly
- Before cooking your rice use only the rice measuring cup for measuring your rice. Transfer the rice to a sieve and rinse under cold running water until the liquid coming from the rice is clear. The starch in the rice can often be the culprit for soggy rice. You can also use a bowl for this, swirling the water around the rice grains and draining, repeat until the water is clear. Then leave the rice to drain for 5 mins to make sure the water has run off .
- There is also the myth that all rice needs washing all of the time, this is actually not correct as it depends on how the rice has been processed or even the age of the grain. If you find after washing/rinsing the rice, you are still getting rice that is too sticky or dry, then try a batch without rinsing and see how it turns out – if it cooks ok, you have a batch of rice that doesn't need rinsing!
- We always find that the first cook of a new batch of rice is a learning experience – judge how the cooked rice is, if it's too soft you need slightly less water next time (3-4mm less) and if it's too hard you need slightly more water (again, 3-4mm).

Fill with water to the correct level line
- Put the rice into the rice cooker and fill the bowl to the relevant line with fresh, cold water. We always fill to the bottom of the indicated line rather than the top - the less water there is in the machine during cooking the less sticky and soft the rice will be - a very precise way of doing things, but it works. If you prefer softer rice then fill to the top of the line.

Release the steam
- Once the cooker has swtiched to KEEP WARM, open the lid, give the rice a good stir with the spatula to release any excess water and to break any clumps of rice which may have formed and then leave on KEEP WARM for maybe 30 minutes.
- A good premium rice cooker should never produce stodgy rice. Instead you get perfect fluffy rice as the end product. By following the above tips and troubleshooting you can achieve good rice every time.
- Note that most Japanese style digital rice cookers are designed to produce rice that clumps together but also produces distinct grains when broken apart. Following the tips above with the rinsing and choosing the correct type of grain will help to produce more 'Indian style' basmati rice with distinct grains.

SLOW COOK AND STEAMING GUIDE

SLOW COOKING

A rice cooker can be used for so much more than rice and grains. Some rice cookers have a SLOW COOK function which can replace your traditional slow cooker – **the benefit of using a rice cooker as a slow cooker is because it is a sealed unit and very heat efficient.** Your food cooks faster but still at that low tenderising heat and the flavour/juices get retained or reabsorbed. The slow cook setting can be used for cooking full joints of meat, soups or casseroles/stews. It's a versatile function that can be used for lentils/beans making cooking them easier. For slow cook recipes you an literally throw in all the ingredients at the start and let the slow cooking do the work.

Slow Cooking Meats/Joints

Pork
You can cook pork with just seasoning, or you use a spice rub which is great for pulled pork.

Spice Rub:
1 tbsp ground black pepper
1-2 tbsp cayenne pepper
2 tbsp chili powder
2 tbsp ground cumin
2 tbsp dark brown sugar
1 tbsp dried oregano
4 tbsp paprika
2 tbsp table salt
1 tbsp granulated sugar
1 tbsp ground white pepper

Massage the spice rub into the pork and leave it for at least 3 hours. Put the pork into the inner bowl and cook for 6-8 hours - the longer the better. Once cooked, shred the pork joint with two forks and add barbeque sauce.

 NOTE For **Fish** it is better to use the STEAM function (see table below) rather than the SLOW COOK function as it prevents drying out.

Beef
Season the beef well on all sides with salt and pepper. Place the beef inside the inner bowl and cook for 4-6 hours on the slow cook setting depending on how large the joint is and how well you want the beef done.

Don't open the lid too many times! This applies to all meat slow cooking. The more you open the lid the more the flavourful moisture used to cook the meat will escape.

Chicken
Whole chickens are usually too large to fit into a rice cooker inner bowl, but you can cook chicken breasts, chicken thighs (bone in or out) or legs on the slow cook setting. Cook for 1-2 hours depending on how much chicken you are cooking. The bigger the amount, the longer you have to leave the meat to SLOW COOK.

Use a marinade or a spice rub on the chicken and place inside the inner bowl with some chopped up vegetables on the bottom, you can then shred the chicken with two forks and use in a salad, quesadillas, burritos, wraps. A simple and tasty trick.

Soups/Casseroles/Stews
These dishes can be cooked in a pan can also be cooked using the SLOW COOK function of a rice cooker. Create heart warming soups such as chicken and pearl barley or minestrone, stews such as a Moroccan and chickpea delight. You can also use the SLOW COOK function to make tender flavourful dishes such as our recipes for chilli con carne or beef goulash.

STEAMING

Some rice cookers have a steaming function and you can usually use it as a stand alone steamer (use 1.5-2 cups of water in the inner bowl) or you can cook rice at the same time as steaming food. If steaming whilst cooking rice, you use the rice function for the type of rice you are cooking and add the steaming basket to the inner bowl above the rice. Cooking rice and steaming at the same time is a quick and easy way to prepare full, healthy meals. Here are estimated cooking times for different types of food using the 'STEAM' function.

INGREDIENTS	AMOUNT	COOKING TIME	TIPS FOR STEAMING
Carrot	200g/1pcs	20 mins	Cut into bite size pieces
Broccoli	200g	15 mins	Cut into bite size pieces
Spinach	100g	15 mins	Cut into bite size pieces
Pumpkin	250g	20 mins	Cut into bite size pieces
Potato	450g	40 mins	Cut into bite size pieces
Sweet Potato	300g	35 mins	Cut into bite size pieces
Corn	200g	30 mins	Cut into bite size pieces
Chicken	200g/1 fillet	30 mins	Make cuts on side touching the steam basket
Fish (white fish & salmon)	150g	20 mins	Slice to less than 2cm and wrap in foil
Prawn & Scallops	15pcs/150g	20 mins	Prawns - steam without removing shells Scallops - remove from shell
Refrigerated Meat Dumpling	200g	15 mins	Leave space between food
Frozen Meat Dumpling	200g	20 mins	Cut into bite size pieces

REMEMBER - if you steam at the same time as cooking rice that the maximum capacity of rice you can cook decreases. There will be guidance in your rice cooker manual for how much rice you can cook and steam at the same time. If you cook rice and steam at the same time, you can open the lid (very carefully, minding the steam that is released from the unit) to **add the steaming basket part way through the cooking cycle so the vegetables are not over-cooked.**

INDEX

INDEX

HAPPY
COOKING

BE PART OF OUR RICE COOKER

REVOLUTION

www.yum-asia.com

Printed in Great Britain
by Amazon

17604357R00080